Pragmatism as humanism
The philosophy of William James

Pragmatism as humanism

The philosophy of William James

Patrick Kiaran Dooley

Professional/Technical Series
Nelson-Hall nh Chicago

ISBN 0-88229-125-4

Library of Congress Catalog Card No. 73-86935

Copyright © 1974 by Patrick Kiaran Dooley

Manufactured in the United States of America

jwe   3-30-83

To
my Mother and Father

Contents

Preface		**xi**
1.	**Introduction**	**1**
2.	**"Man" in James' psychological thought**	**11**

James' views on a scientific study of man
   Scope of psychology
   Methods of psychology
   Nature of psychology
An interactionist view of man
   Attractiveness of the mind/body parallelism view
     of man
   Reasons for an interactionist view of man
The stream of consciousness
   Every thought is part of personal consciousness
   Consciousness is constantly changing
   Consciousness is sensibly continuous
   Consciousness deals with objects independent
     of itself
   Consciousness is selective
The selectivity of consciousness according to
   interests
   Sensation and perception of things

Perception of reality: belief
Conception and reasoning
Emotion
Instinct
Voluntary action

3. **"Man" in James' ethical and religious thought**   **61**
    "Man" in James' ethical thought: "the
        essentials of an ethical universe"
    Metaphysical question—possibility of moral
        experience
    Psychological question—origin and nature of
        moral ideals
    Casuistic question—society, religion, and the
        individual
    "Man" in the religious thought of James
    Nature and legitimacy of belief: Nature of belief.
        Legitimacy of belief.
    Effects of religious belief: an examination of the
        religious propensity in man: Primal religious
        sentiment. Conversion—gradual and sudden.
        Effect of conversion: an evaluation of sainthood.
        Mysticism and natural theology as warrants for
        the unseen world.

4. **James' humanistic epistemology and metaphysics 115**
    James' pragmatic humanism
    James' pragmatic theory of meaning
    Pragmatism as a theory of truth: James' theory of
        truth as a development of his philosophy of man.
        James' theory of truth as a "humanism."
    James' radical empiricism
    Radical empiricism: an epistemology of pure
        experience: Reality as pure experience and per-
        ceptual knowledge. Conceptual knowledge as

*ministerial to perceptual knowledge. Experience
and the existence of the self.*
*Radical empiricism: a pluralistic universe: Our
experience of activity. Pluralism versus monism.
A melioristic universe. A finite God.*

5. **"Humanism" as a unifying theme in James'
   philosophy**   163
   James' theory of man
   James' philosophy as a "humanism"
   The "whole man" as a guide to inquiry
   James' theory of truth as a "humanism"
   *Human experiences as revelatory of the nature
   of reality*
   *Philosophy as an articulation of the human
   perspective*
   The dignity of man in James' philosophy

List of abbreviations   181
Notes   183
Bibliography   203
Index   215

Preface

Of late there has been a mini-renaissance of American philosophy, especially of interest in William James' *The Principles of Psychology* and *The Varieties of Religious Experience* as anticipations and examples of phenomenology. As in the past, aspects of James' thought are being studied without reference to the over-arching themes and positions of his philosophy. This study provides that larger context.

James has always been praised for his insightfulness and cursed for his lack of continuity and consistency. In the minds of some, James made several philosophical re-starts and to understand him the reader must also wipe clean the slate and begin again. I have attempted to articulate and defend the unity and coherence of James' philosophical vision. The central insight of his thought is his theory of man, his humanism. This view of man is first explicated in his very early psychological and ethical works and provides the key to understanding his later metaphysical and epistemological pragmatism. My study is generally sympathetic and my view of the overall cogency and defensibility of James' philosophy is not, I hope, generated by a faulty "sentiment of rationality."

Very many people have helped in all of this; several deserve special mention. A large debt is owed to members of the philosophy department of the University of Notre Dame, especially Dr. C. F. Delaney who introduced me to William James and helped me through the initial version.

Financial support has been provided by a Schmitt Foundation Dissertation Fellowship and by a College of Finger Lakes Consortium Research Grant which allowed me to spend parts of two summers reading the James' papers at Harvard's Houghton Library. Gratitude is also due a very efficient and helpful typist, Miss Noreen Melillo. Finally, for much help and more encouragement, a thank you to my wife, Nora.

1
Introduction

T he principal objective of this study is to provide a thematic exposition of the philosophy of William James. James himself suggests the unifying theme of his thought when he refers to his philosophy as a "humanism." It is my contention that this term, "humanism," was a carefully chosen one, and if respected, will provide the proper focus for understanding and unifying his thought.

For James, "humanism" involved the admission that "it is impossible to strip the *human element* out from even our most abstract theorizing,"[1] and that consequently, "to an unascertainable extent our truths are man-made products."[2] A proper appreciation of what James means by "the human element" involves understanding his theory of man and his position on the nature of human experience. The position to be defended, then, is that James' theory of man is the fulcrum of his philosophy and the key to a unified understanding of his thought.

Quite simply, James' theory of man in its unifying ramifications has been overlooked in Jamesian research. I view this study as an attempt to fill that gap by an exposition of his theory of man and by a discussion of that theory as the philosophical basis for his mature metaphysics and epistemology.

This approach to James' thought has the merit of being unstrained and natural, for it follows the chronological development of his thought as he moved from anatomy to psychology to philosophy. Further, this treatment of James gives what I feel to be the proper estimation of the importance of his works prior to the publication of *Pragmatism* in 1907. In fact, most of my attention will be directed toward his psychological works (*The Principles of Psychology*, 1890 and *Psychology*, 1892) and to what he calls his works in "popular philosophy" (*The Will to Believe*, 1897 and *The Varieties of Religious Experience*, 1902) for it is in these early works that James develops his theory of man. Finally, I hold that this stress of his early works and the theory of man contained therein is warranted, for it supplies both the direction and the philosophical background for his mature metaphysics and epistemology. Even more strongly, it is my contention that James' philosophy is essentially a philosophy of man—a *humanism*.

The study then has two general tasks: an exposition of James' theory of man (chaps. 2 and 3), and a discussion of that theory of man in relation to his mature thought (chap. 4). The final chapter will summarize his theory of man and discuss humanism as a unifying theme.

In the second chapter, James' psychological analysis of man will be examined. There we will see that James tentatively accepts an interactionist view of man while arguing that the empirically given selectivity of consciousness and the instrumental character of human knowing support that view of man. In the third chapter I will analyze James' treatment of the ethical and religious experiences of the "whole man." There he discovers additional support for an interactionist

view of man and concludes that the selectivity of consciousness can account for man's moral experiences of freedom and
impugnability, as well as for man's religious experiences.
Hence James' philosophy from 1878 to 1907 is a humanism
insofar as he is exclusively concerned with framing a theory
of man.

In the fourth chapter it will be argued that James' mature
philosophy provides us with two additional, yet interrelated
senses in which his philosophy is a humanism. First of all,
his own distinctive interpretation of pragmatism (which he
calls "humanism") is based on and is a direct development
of, his psychological, ethical and religious analyses of the
nature of man. Secondly, in his metaphysics, James argues
that a view of the world consonant with the demands of the
"whole man" and true to our experience of the world,
holds that the world is open, unfinished and undetermined.
In such a melioristic, pluralistic world, man determines the
future of the world through the exercise of his freedom. In
this mature metaphysics then, James articulates humanism in
the classical sense of conceiving man as the center of the
whole of things. In the fifth chapter, I will draw together the
various strands of James' theory of man and discuss the
various facets of his humanism as a unifying theme. But
before turning to the specifics of James' theory of man, a few
preliminary general remarks on the nature of James' thought
and two terminological clarifications are necessary.

Although James is recognized as a brilliant and seminal
mind, he is also notorious for his vague and unsystematic
thought. Gordon Allport aptly characterizes the typical reaction to reading James:

At first, led along by lucidity and inspiration he (the
reader) finds himself assenting eagerly to a great many
discrete observations, as arresting in their brilliance as

anything he ever encountered. But soon he comes upon propositions that contradict one another and do violence to his sense of syllogism.[3]

Part of the looseness and vagueness of James' thought can be attributed to a fact characteristic of his published works: all of his works except *The Principles of Psychology* and its abridgement, *Psychology*, were either published lectures (*The Will to Believe, Human Immortality, Talks to Teachers, The Varieties of Religious Experience, Pragmatism, A Pluralistic Universe*) or collected articles (*The Meaning of Truth, Essays in Radical Empiricism*). He often expressed the hope of doing a tight, systematic work; after the publication of *The Varieties of Religious Experience* he remarks: "I want now, if possible, to write something serious, systematic and syllogistic, I've had enough of the squashy popular-lecture style."[4] Yet only six years later he agreed to give the Hibbert Lectures at Manchester College, Oxford (published as *A Pluralistic Universe*). In a letter to Schiller he once again expressed the same reluctance with the popular-lecture style:

I actually *hate* lecturing; and this job (the Hibbert Lectures) condemns me to publish another book written in picturesque and popular style when I was settling down to something whose manner should be more *strengwissenschaftlich*, i.e., concise, dry, and impersonal. My free and easy style in *Pragmatism* has made me so many enemies in academic and pedantic circles that I hate to go on increasing their number, and want to become tighter instead of looser.[5]

The book he speaks of sitting down to write was never finished. In a memorandum directing that it be published (*Some Problems in Philosophy*, 1911) he wrote: "Say it is fragmentary and unfinished . . . call it 'a beginning of an introduction to philosophy.' Say that I hoped to round out my system, which now is too much like an arch built only on one side."[6] Accordingly, one could argue that while James wanted to be a "philosopher's" philosopher, his considerable renown made him an unwilling captive of "popular" philosophy. This interpretation is lent support by his well-known characterization of the "tough-and-tender-minded" types of thinking. James' own oscillation between these two tendencies (objective and neutral versus subjective and interested) will form a subtheme in our study.

Perhaps a more accurate assessment of the looseness in James' thought would be that he felt an aversion for strict, rigorous thinking. He writes in a letter to James Ward, shortly after the publication of *Psychology*:

Yes I am too unsystematic and loose! But in this case (the writing of *Psychology*) I permitted myself to remain so deliberately on account of the strong aversion with which I am filled for the humbugging pretence of exactitude in the definition of terms and description of states that has prevailed in psychological literature.[7]

His aversion to logical, systematic, rigorous thought was grounded in his conviction that the real is infinitely richer than the logical:

Thought deals . . . solely with surfaces. It can name the thickness of reality, but it cannot fathom it and its *insufficiency here is essential and permanent, not temporary*. The only way in which to apprehend reality's thickness is either to experience it directly by being a part of reality one's self or to evoke it in imagination by sympathetically divining some one else's inner life.[8]

James felt that reality was richer than a tight, systematic conceptualization of it and accordingly he valued a direct acquaintance with the paradoxical character of reality over logical consistency. In his preface to the Italian edition of *The Principles of Psychology*, he wrote that he has:

> expressly avoided the outward appearance of doctrine and system, the definitions, classifications, subdivisions and multiplication of technical terms, because I know that these things tend to substitute an artificial schematism for the living reality with which I wished to bring my reader into direct concrete acquaintance.[9]

Nonetheless working with James' thought is not all that hopeless. Yet it is important to be aware of the character of his works. He is not one who begins with strict definitions and proceeds systematically through an argument. Instead, he begins by giving a descriptive account of many examples and, given that *context*, he gradually draws out generalizations and conclusions. Hence, it is particularly risky to give a strict analysis of one of James' arguments without first establishing the context from which its definitions are drawn, and upon which the argument rests. Yet often even after extreme care is taken to let James speak for himself, his thought is not amenable to strict analysis. However, we have found that much of James' infamous vagueness and looseness can be alleviated if his treatment of specific problems is placed in the proper matrix. That matrix is his theory of man. We will show, for example, that many of the criticisms of his most troublesome positions (e.g., the will to believe, his humanistic pragmatism, and the problem of the existence of the self) have been misreadings of James for the simple reason that these positions were not viewed in the proper context—his theory of man. We are not suggesting that James is a perfectly consistent and coherent thinker; he is not. We do, however, hold that much of his alleged looseness and inconsistency is, if not eliminated, at least lessened if his theory of man is allowed to form the context for his treatment of specific problems. We suggest then, that his thought is more readily understood and more adequately evaluated when viewed in the context of the central concern of his thought—his humanism.

One final note on terminology is in order. James continually uses two notions—"the whole man" and "an interactionist view of man"—in his theory of man. Neither notion is strictly defined. Although we have attempted to let James work out definitions of these notions as he develops his philosophy of man, a few comments at the outset may be of help.

James uses the term "whole man" as a caution against the adoption of an artificially narrow concept of man. He argues, for example, if our notion of man is based only upon a consideration of man's practical experiences, we will distort our notion of man. In his article, "Remarks on Spencer's Definition of Mind,"[10] he maintains that Spencer's notion of the human mind is inadequate for he only defines mind in reference to man's most basic practical, survival-orientated needs. James grants that in response to those basic needs the mind functions in order to ascertain outward fact, but he argues that the mind functions in response to other needs as well:

mind as we actually find it, contains all sorts of laws—those of logic, those of fancy, of wit, of taste, decorum, beauty, morals and so forth as well as perception of fact. . . survival is only one out of many interests. . . . What are these interests? Most men would reply that they are all that makes survival worth securing. The

social affections, all the various forms of play, the thrill-
ing intimations of art, the delights of philosophic contemplation, the rest of religious emotion, the joy of moral
self-approbation, the charm of fancy and of wit.[11]

James, then, holds that an adequate notion of mind must take
into account all the various forms of mental activity. Hence,
when James refers to the demands or the exigencies or the
experiences of the "whole man,"[12] he has in mind a notion of
man which includes all the desires and interests of man, be
they practical, aesthetic, ethical, or religious. Hence, the
"whole man" is James' way of referring to his position that
the totality and variety of human experiences must be in-
corporated into an adequate concept of man.

James refers to his theory of man as an "interactionist
view of man." At the outset of his psychology, he argues
that if our experience of our conscious states positing ends
and guiding behavior in view of those ends is to be accepted
as genuine, an interactionist view of man in which consciousness is efficacious, is requisite. He defines an interactionist view of man only in reference to a parallelist view
of man. The particular parallelist view of man he specifically
refers to is the conscious automaton theory which holds that
consciousness is an impotent epiphenomenon, which merely
accompanies purely neural processes. James argues that if our
concept of man is not to be distorted, we must opt for an
interactionist view of man in which consciousness is causally
efficacious in directing behavior. Although it is clear that in
an interactionist view of man *consciousness is efficacious*, it is
not clear what interacts nor precisely how consciousness is
efficacious. In other words, the whole notion "an interactionist view of man in which consciousness is efficacious"
is only defined in reference to the whole notion "a conscious automaton theory view of man in which consciousness

is an impotent epiphenomenon"; the individual terms in neither of the notions are defined. In the development of this theory of man James attempts to specify what he means by the individual terms in his view of man. However, at the outset, he simply speaks of the "things" which interact as "mental life" and "bodily life." In his discussion of the above-mentioned theories of man he uses a variety of terms to refer to "mental life" and "bodily life"—for the former, "consciousness," "conscious states," "mind," "soul," "psychical states," and "spirit"; for the latter, "brain," "body," "physical states," "nerve processes," "matter." He only specifies "consciousness" or "conscious states" by saying that they are "the phenomena . . . we call feelings, desires, cognitions, reasonings, decisions, and the like."[13] Hence, although James has not determined *which* "things" interact or *how* they interact, he provisionally adopts at the outset an interactionist view of man in which consciousness is efficacious in directing behavior. In the pages that follow we will discuss James' attempts to specify this view of man.

2

"Man" in James' psychological thought

Since we propose that James' theory of man provides a theme for properly understanding and unifying his thought, our treatment of James will focus on two considerations: a discussion of his theory of man (our second and third chapters) and a discussion of the metaphysics consonant with this view of man (our fourth chapter). The present chapter considers the theory of man developed in his psychological works—*The Principles of Psychology* (1890) and *Psychology* (1892).[1]

We begin this chapter with James' discussion of the methods and nature of a scientific study of man—i.e., his view of a psychology of man. Our second section examines his commitment to a psychosomatic view of man. James argues for a mind/body interactionism in which consciousness is efficacious. The remainder of this chapter considers "the efficacy of consciousness." The third section deals with James' analysis of the five characteristics of consciousness and the fourth, his discussion of the mechanism of consciousness's efficacity—interested selection. Put another way, this chapter traces James' grappling with a single, critical question: can or should a scientific study of man be a metaphysically neutral endeavor? After considerable vacillation he answers in the negative. As we shall see later, the reasons offered in defense of this particular stance provide in a germinal way the outlines of his mature philosophy of humanism.

JAMES' VIEWS ON A SCIENTIFIC STUDY OF MAN

In June of 1878 (the year James' course in psychology was transferred from the physiology to the philosophy department) he signed a contract to write a psychology for Henry Holt's "American Science Series." James declined to try to complete the book in one year but he agreed to finish it by 1880. The two-year period proved unrealistic—it was not until 1890 that the proofs were in Holt's hands with this assessment from James:

> No one could be more disgusted than I at the sight of this book. *No* subject is worth being treated in 1000 pages [actually 1400 pages]. Had I the time I could rewrite it in 500; but as it stands it is this or nothing—a loathsome, distended, tumefied, bloated, dropsical mass, testifying to nothing but two facts: first, that there is no such thing as a *science* of psychology and second, that W. J. is an incapable.[2]

History did not concur in James' assessment. It was an enormously popular and influential book. Historians of psychology generally agree that the *Principles* ushered in the new, "scientific" psychology as an independent discipline.

On the contrary, James' own methodological reflections on a scientific study of man indicate a variety of reasons for psychology remaining subordinate to a set of philosophical commitments. We will examine briefly James' views on the scope and methods of psychology before concentrating on his position on the nature of psychology.

Scope of psychology

James begins the *Principles* with the following definition: "Psychology is the science of mental life, both its phenomena and their conditions."[3] He observes that as a natural science, psychology will attempt an empirical correlation of the phenomena of thought and feeling with specific brain states. For example, even if there be a soul (and thought one of its faculties) this faculty does not exist absolutely but it works under bodily conditions; hence, the psychologist must still attempt to discover and correlate these bodily conditions with thought. In general, this correlation amounts to discovering how the brain is the immediate bodily condition of thought and feeling.

There is a second area of investigation for psychology. Not only are mental phenomena antecedently conditioned *a parte ante* by bodily (brain) processes, but mental phenomena evoke subsequently bodily responses and promote certain behavior, *a parte post*. James states as a general law, "No mental modification ever occurs which is not accompanied or followed by a bodily change."[4] Therefore, the second area for empirical study in psychology is the description and analysis of bodily reactions and human behavior. It is paradoxical, but not surprising, that while insisting on making psychology a natural science (i.e., an experimental study of the *a parte ante* brain states—reaction times, spans of attention, retentiveness of memory, study of paralysis and brain damage, etc.) James makes his most distinctive contributions in the area of analysis and description of the *a parte post* bodily and behavioral responses.

Psychology, then, is the science of "mental life." While noting that the boundary line of "mental" is vague, James offers these suggestions. He begins with Herbert Spencer's formula that the essence of mental life is the "adjustment" of inner to outer relations. Mental life intervenes between the impressions from outer relations (the world) and the reactions of the inner (the body). The nature of the mind's intervention consists in guiding activity toward an end. However, blind pursuance of an end will not qualify; rather, "the pursuance of future ends and the *choice* of means for attainment are the mark and criterion of the presence of mentality."[5] In other words, mentality is present when there is consciousness of error and subsequent adjustment to another means to accomplish the end.

Thus James holds that psychology as a natural science will study mental life by correlating the thoughts and feelings with the body. At this stage he only attempts a characterization of mental life as that activity which guides and corrects actions in view of an end. Thoughts and feelings (the phenomena of mental life) will be correlated either in terms of the brain conditions of thoughts and feelings, *a parte ante* or the bodily reactions and behavior mental life evoke, *a parte post*.

Methods of psychology

There are three methods at the disposal of the psychologist: experimental, introspective, and comparative. James considers all three useful.

James describes the experimental method by reference to the "microscopic psychology" of the Germans Weber, Fechner, Vierodt, and Wundt. These "new psychologists" attempt to study mental life by reducing it to quantitative scales. Typical areas of experimentation include the correlation of sensations with outer stimuli, the measurement of the accuracy of memory, and examination of elementary laws of obliviscence and retention. James feels this method has inherent limitations[6] but is valuable since its factual, empirical orientation discourages unwarranted speculation.

The method of the old psychology is *introspection*. James regards as the most fundamental postulate of psychology that we have inward mental states, that we are aware of them and that "these inward mental states are different from all other objects with which we cognitively deal."[7] Our access to these mental states is via introspection.

The introspective access is neither infallible, nor worthless. It is one of the varieties of the psychologist's fallacy to claim *immediate* consciousness of mental states. A thought is aware of its object and is not aware of itself: "no subjective state, whilst present is its own object; its object is always something else."[8] Thus our introspective access is not immediate but *reflexive*. Introspection is just as fallible as any other form of observation and the only test, for it is the empirical one of future experience.

Finally, the *comparative* method, James sees as an overflow of Darwinian enthusiasm. Studies of instincts of animals, reasoning faculties of bees and ants, studies of the minds of savages, madmen, and infants, are used to supplement the first two methods. Although James praises the gain in information which the comparative method can provide, he warns of the difficulty of interpreting its data.

In the *Principles*, James most frequently uses the introspective method. He points out, however, that the comparative and experimental methods are important since the use of *observation* gives psychology a factual, empirical orientation and indicates that psychology need not be restricted to a "first person," introspective study.

Nature of psychology

Although, as was noted above, historians of psychology regard the *Principles* as initiating the era of psychology as an independent, natural science, James himself was convinced that psychology should not and could not be a metaphysically neutral science. Since James was by profession a natural scientist (he began his career in biology and anatomy, and only later turned to philosophy), his aversion for the new scientific psychologies (he calls Wundt, Weber, etc., "the new prism, pendulum and chronograph philosophers"[9]), cannot be written off as the prejudice of a philosopher against natural science. Indeed, James offers three reasons why the new, scientific psychologies cannot supplant the old, philosophical psychologies.

First, the investigations and hypotheses of the new experimental psychologists have been suggested by the old introspective psychologies. In an article on Ferrier's *The Function of the Brain*, James argues that the laboratory experiments of the brain physiologists are "mere hypothetical schematizations, in material terms, of the laws which introspection has long ago laid bare."[10] The old psychology cannot be abandoned, for its insights suggest the experimentally profitable hypotheses.

Second, the experimental results of the new psychology are meaningless unless interpreted:

Physiological-psychology is really nothing but a collection of experimental investigations, set apart for convenient study, but quite unable of leading to any general conclusions without interpretation. And in the interpretations, all the problems and difficulties of the "older" psychologies come up afresh and its "speculative" methods have to be used again.[11]

In an earlier (1878) lecture he had made this point more simply:

> The subjective method (introspection) has not only given us almost all our fundamentally secure psychological knowledge, but has suggested all of our interpretations of the facts of brain-physiology.[12]

The raw facts of the new psychology must be interpreted and the old psychology has the proper tools of introspection and analysis. Put another way, the new psychologies are not going to solve the old problems (soul/body, mind/brain, personal identity) by substituting for them new problems which can be dealt with rigorously. The old problems will reappear at a deeper level and will still require the methods of the old philosophical psychology.

The third reason stems from the notion of cause. James feels that unless the new psychology gets beyond description and statistical correlation to causal explanation (as understood by the old psychologies) it will not become a science. In answer to James Ward's review of the *Principles*, James writes:

> The real thing to aim at is a causal account; and I must say that appears to lie (provisionally, at least) in the region of the laws as yet unknown of the connection of the mind with the body. There is the subject for a "science" of psychology.[13]

Although at this juncture, James seems to mean by *cause* "inwardly creating or engendering effects" he later speaks of the mind/body causal connection in terms of "transmission or permission."[14] Since James does little more than rely on the common sense notion of cause as "source of change" this charge that the new psychologies have not become "scientific" remains largely rhetorical.

James' own position on the nature of psychology undergoes the following transformation. The official stance of the *Principles* is that it was to be a positivistic psychology, free from metaphysical speculation, utilizing the comparative, experimental, and introspective methods. (In fact, James states in the preface of the *Principles* that this positivistic point of view is the only feature of the book for which he wishes to claim originality.) In the preface of the Italian translation of the *Principles*, James articulates this stance:

> I thought that by frankly putting psychology in the position of a natural science, eliminating certain metaphysical questions from its scope altogether, confining myself to what could be immediately verified by everyone's own consciousness, a central mass of experience could be described which everyone might accept no matter what the differing ulterior philosophic interpretations of it might be.[15]

Thus, James remarks that even though the soul may exist and may be the hypothesis which is most salutary, psychology need not assume the soul. Or, that psychology as a science can safely posit determinism even if free will be true.

However, later in the same preface, James indicates his change of mind:

> But I confess that . . . I have become more and more convinced of the difficulty of treating psychology without introducing *some true and suitable philosophical doctrine*.[16]

James' mature position on the nature of psychology is that even though a metaphysically neutral psychology is impossible, psychology ought to be a provisional endeavor, based on *data* which can be verified in everyone's consciousness, and *interpretations* which clearly exhibit their metaphysical presuppositions. Moreover, and most importantly, a "true and suitable metaphysical doctrine" will be one which can accommodate the demands of the "whole man," i.e., man's ethical, aesthetic, and religious demands. While these demands are not fully articulated nor are their metaphysical presuppositions fully worked out in psychology, psychology ought to offer explanations which can accommodate these demands. For instance, psychology may assume determinism, but it can also offer a viable hypothesis for freedom.

In sum, James' methodological reflections on the nature of psychology gives us an indication of what we can expect in our analysis of his psychological study of man. We have learned that he considers psychology to be the study of mental life (characterized by him as a guiding and corrective activity in view of an end) which attempts to discover the bodily conditions and consequences of the phenomena of mental life—thoughts and feelings. This suggests that James seeks a scientific, "empirical," that is, a metaphysically neutral "new" psychology. However, he holds that psychology as a practical study of the "whole man" must not abandon the methods and problems of the "old" psychology. In short, he concludes that a metaphysical doctrine which can accommodate man's aesthetic, ethical, and religious experiences, must be introduced; hence a metaphysically neutral psychology is impossible. In a germinal way then, James' methodological reflections on the nature of psychology as a science expresses our thesis. James holds a very definite view of the nature of man; this view of man is operative in his position on the nature of psychology as the scientific study of man. Hence, James has permitted the demands of the whole man, a stance chosen on the basis of extrascientific, philosophical grounds, to dictate his position on the nature of a science of psychology. The demands of the "whole man" also influence his choice of a particular psychological account of man and to that we now turn.

AN INTERACTIONIST VIEW OF MAN

James notes that since "man" can be described in terms of either bodily or mental language, psychology must, at the outset, consider the various views of man—e.g., what are the general views of man in terms of the interrelation of mental and bodily life? James argues that the psychologist must opt for one of two concepts of man: a mind/body parallelism or a psychosomatic interactionism. In this section we will examine James' discussion of the attractiveness of the parallelist theory and analyze the reasons why he decided in favor of the interactionist view of man. Notice that James argues that the two theories differ in their concept of consciousness ("impotent epiphenomenon" or "efficacious phenomenon") and also that the "whole man" notion once again is central.

Attractiveness of the mind/body parallelism view of man

As late as 1879, James was disposed to accept the current parallelist view of man—the conscious automaton theory. This account of man's behavior relies on a single explanatory framework, the stimulus/response account. It argues that if certain of our actions (reflex acts) are unconscious, the principle of continuity urges that our more complicated acts (conscious actions) also be explained by the stimulus/response paradigm—the only difference being that "conscious" actions involve the neural centers of the hemispheres. He puts it in this way: "As actions of a certain degree of complexity are brought about by the mere mechanism, why may not actions of still greater degree of complexity be the result of a more refined mechanism?"[17] In this view, consciousness is an impotent epiphenomenon: "feeling is a mere collateral product of our nervous system processes."[18] Besides observing the principle of continuity in nature and thereby offering a single explanatory framework, James felt that the conscious-automaton theory of man offered more promise to psychology as a natural science for two reasons: it avoids the mind/body "chasm," and psychology's task could then be confined to an empirical study of the stimulus/response mechanism. James felt the persuasiveness of these reasons but rejected the theory because it distorted our concept of man.

The suspicion arises that the automaton theory may be a distortion of the facts (i.e., human behavior) to be explained because it opposes our common sense view of things. We lose all naturalness of speech, and we must abandon the deliverances of introspection if we hold that feelings, ideas, and motives have no influence in our behavior, but only *accompany* purely neural actions and reactions. James argues that it is important that psychology, whenever possible, retain the common sense point of view since much of psychology at least begins with an analysis of ordinary language; moreover, an analysis of the common sense deliverance of introspection has directed psychological inquiry by suggesting most of the hypotheses of the "new" laboratory psychology.

Reasons for an interactionist view of man

James offers a variety of reasons for a psychosomatic view of man in which there is mental/physical interaction since consciousness is efficacious. He calls his sorts first reasons "*a priori* presumptive evidence."[19] Consciousness is present in the more highly developed organisms. According to the principle of natural selection if consciousness has no purpose, it should not have survived; hence consciousness must be of some use to the higher organisms. In the lower, unconscious life forms, a rigidly determined nervous system reacts infallibly to given stimuli, but it is powerless to react to novel data. On the contrary, in the higher, conscious life forms nervous systems are unstable and a variety of responses are available. In fact, if the consciousness of the higher organisms would not be efficacious in selecting and guiding one of the possible reactions as beneficial, the higher organisms would be *biologically less suited* for survival than the mechanically determined, lower organisms. James reasons that the role of consciousness appears to consist in loading the dice in favor of the survival of the less determined organisms.

Consciousness's loading the dice in favor of the survival will amount to its selecting responses congruent with the interests of the organism, e.g., "useful discharge," "appropriate direction," "right reaction," "beneficial interaction with environment." But without consciousness, these normative judgments are meaningless; in fact, even "survival" makes no sense without consciousness. Until you posit consciousness, *survival* remains an hypothesis:

> Now the important thing is to notice that the goal cannot be posited at all as long as we consider the purely physical order of existence. Matter has no ideals. It must be entirely indifferent to the molecules C, H, N, and O, whether they combine in a live body or a dead one.[20]

A judgment of comparison requires a *tertium quid* where the two states of affairs meet on equal terms. The forum for comparison is consciousness. "Every actually existing consciousness seems to itself at any rate to be a fighter for ends, . . . but for its presence, (there) would be no ends at all."[21] Thus the a priori reasons for the efficacity of consciousness are that consciousness establishes ends and by its selection, chooses means to those ends.

A *posteriori*, there is circumstantial evidence that consciousness is present "as an organ added for the sake of steering a nervous system grown too complex to regulate itself."[22] Here James argues by examples. First, consciousness is most noticeable when the nerve processes are hesitant. Habitual actions become unconscious but when we attempt to break a habit or are forced to change our responses to deal with novel data, consciousness is at its peak: "where indecision is great, as before a dangerous leap, consciousness is agonizingly intense."[23] Secondly, it is not mere coincidence that pleasures are generally beneficial and pains detrimental. Spencer argues that if pleasures were detrimental to the organism, natural selection would soon render the organism extinct. Granted, but what still remains unexplained (unless you opt for an a priori harmony) is *why* pains indicate processes injurious to the organism. James' point is that these remarkable coincidences of pleasure—good, and pain—injury, indicate the plausibility of the efficacy of the conscious states we call pleasure and pain. Finally, consciousness takes cognizance of functional errors and exerts corrective pressures. Conscious organisms do not mechanically repeat an errant reaction, but they substitute correct ones or in some cases, another part will take up the function of the part lost.

James also favored the interactionist view of man because he felt that the parallelism of the automaton theory evaded causal explanation. Discriminating and labeling states of mind and correlating them with specific nerve centers is only the descriptive stage of science. Psychology will become a science only when it crosses the psychophysical chasm and explains how mind states and nerve centers interact. James confesses his inability to explain how the psychical and the physical interact, but he does indicate that the scientific desideratum ought to be a causal explanation of this inter- action. We notice here again James only alludes to what he means by "causal explanation" and leaves us with a sketchy, unfinished statement.

Finally, James' *fundamental reason* for adopting the inter- actionist view of man was that, quite to the contrary of the automaton theory, it did not distort our concept of man. James wanted a psychology of the whole man. The "whole man" he was interested in has certain moral and religious aspirations which consciousness posits as ends and values. These aspirations are only meaningful if man is free, that is, if consciousness is efficacious. The interactionist view is therefore preferable since it can accommodate man's moral and religious desires.

None of the above reasons in favor of the interactionist view is fully persuasive, nor do they together amount to more than presumptive evidence. Accordingly, James' adop- tion of the interactionist view is only provisional. The rea- sons he explicitly gives for so adopting this view are: 1) the psychophysical problem is a metaphysical one and cannot be resolved by psychology; and 2) a metaphysics which can support the interactionist position involves a view of reality in which temporality and novelty are accepted and justified— not explained away. James concludes by saying that he will adopt the common sense interactionist view on this provi- sional basis and that the final justification for the efficacy of consciousness is "pending metaphysical reconstruction not as yet successfully achieved."[24] We too must wait for the full justification of the interactionist view of man, for James'

metaphysical construction is not complete until he writes
A Pluralistic Universe in 1909.

James has given his first indication of the specifics of
his view of man. He opts for a psychosomatic view of man
in which consciousness is efficacious. His reasons for provisionally adopting the common sense interactionist view of
man are based on his contention that psychology as the
study of the "whole man" must be able to accommodate
those experiences in which consciousness posits ends and is
efficacious in directing actions in view of those ends.
Although James postpones his treatment of the "whole man"
(he means here specifically man's conduct in response to
ethical and religious desires), the outlines of his theory of
man are emerging. He views man as an organism in which
mind and body interact by the efficacity of consciousness.

Thus far in this chapter, we have witnessed the following: first, a particular view of the nature of science of
psychology was adopted lest certain experiences of the
"whole man" be explained away. Recall that James found it
necessary to introduce at the outset "some true and suitable
philosophical doctrine."[25] Further, we have seen his rationale
for provisionally adopting a mind/body interactionism in
which consciousness is efficacious. Though biological considerations were conspicuous in his rationale, the crucial
determinant was that an interactionist view was supportive
of the religious and ethical desires of the "whole man." At
this point, James' "scientific" study of man appears to be
largely a rationalization for positions chosen on extrascientific
grounds.

As we shall see in detail, in the fourth chapter, James
contends that the presence and impact of presuppositions is
unavoidable in human knowledge. What must be attempted
therefore, is an honest, explicit statement of the knower's
presuppositions. Further, these presuppositions need not be

blinding; hence science can still be empirical, in the case of psychology, based on data available to anyone's introspection.

We now turn to James' account of those data, the five characteristics of the stream of consciousness.

THE STREAM OF CONSCIOUSNESS

Not only is James' stream of consciousness theory his most outstanding contribution to psychology, it also constitutes the core of his psychological study of the nature of man. His account begins with what he considers to be empirically given: "The first fact for us, then, as psychologists, is that thinking of some sort goes on."[26] Moreover, thinking (or consciousness) is a continually flowing stream, not a train of atomic units (sensations) to be joined together by association or a transcendental ego. James' basic criticism of the classical associationist and transcendentalist theories is that they fail to consult experience. Hume errs by beginning with something which is not given (simple sensations), and he compounds his error by the psychologist's fallacy of substituting the conditions and results of analysis for the real nature and process of the analyzed. What is given is complex, flowing thought, not atomic sensations. Kant continued Hume's error by invoking the agency of the categories working under the transcendental Ego. In James' view the empirically given "passing thought" has among its aspects all the functions and distinctions which supposedly require a transempirical Ego.[27]

The unity Hume and Kant seek is empirically given in the stream of consciousness. For example, if the fact to be known is the sequence of green-followed-by-red-and-their-contrast, we do not have a pure feeling of red, a pure feeling of green and a third unifying feeling which notices red-then-green-but-the-green-was-brighter. Rather what is empirically given in the stream of consciousness is a feeling of pure red in the first segment, followed by a second segment which *is* a feeling of green-following-red-with-the-green-being-brighter. The feelings of qualities in relations are just as much a part of the stream as the feelings of absolute qualities. His summary has that typically Jamesian flair:

> These feelings [of relation] do not cease to be consubstantial with the rest of the stream. . . . They involve no new psychic dimension, as when the transcendentalists, after letting a number of "pure" feelings successively go "bang," bring their *deus ex machina* of an Ego swooping down upon them from his Olympian heights to *make* a cluster of them with his wonderful "relating thought."[28]

Our empirically given starting point is thought-going-on and this thought is not like a train requiring couplings but it is a *continuously flowing stream*. James' analyzes this stream in terms of what he calls the characteristics of consciousness. He discovers five; consciousness is: personal, changing, sensibly continuous, deals with objects independent of itself, and selective.

Every thought is part of personal consciousness

Not only do we have no experience of states of consciousness which are not personal, the only states of consciousness we have access to are *embodied* consciousnesses, in space and time. Thoughts or states of consciousness are not personalized, they *are* personal: "It seems as if the elementary psychic fact were not *thought* or *this thought* or *that thought*, but *my thought*, every thought being owned."[29] (Even the phenomena of subconscious thought, automatic writing, etc., are not instances of nonpersonal thought;

rather, these states of consciousness are parts of secondary selves.) For James, it makes no sense to talk of thoughts or experiences apart from the self; experiences and thoughts are only personal. Since the states of consciousness we study are parts of personal selves, our discussion of the first characteristic of the stream of consciousness becomes a discussion of James' theory of the self.

One analysis of James' theory of the self will be detailed for two reasons, first, his description and account of the self is very insightful and interesting for its own sake, and secondly, it offers us a concrete, pragmatic test case of his claim that his psychology is indeed empirical and scientific. The issue is whether or not to explain the self and its activities by positing a substantial principle, a soul. If James were to allow the interests of the "whole man" free rein, the positing of a soul would be most congenial to man's moral and religious aspirations. But the soul is neither experienced nor does it seem required to explain knowing or personal identity. Precisely at this juncture James will not permit his presuppositions to overrule the evidence of introspection.

James begins his study of the self by noting that ordinarily two aspects of personal existence are discriminated—I and me. The *me* is the self as known, the empirical ego and the *I* is the self as knower, the pure ego. We shall consider the *me* first.

In the *self as known*, it is often hard to distinguish *me* from *mine*; we can, however, generally say that "in its widest possible sense, a man's self (me) is the sum total of all that he can call his."[30] The feelings and actions which our empirical self elicits allows us to distinguish three distinct components of the empirical me: the material, social and spiritual me. James does a masterful phenomenological description of these various mes; we must be content with a sketch.

The first of the empirical mes is the *material me*. The things I can call me or mine range over my body, my family, my home, my possessions. In short, the material me consists in *things* I appropriate. The *social me* consists in the recognition I seek and gain from my mates. There are obviously as many social mes as the number of various roles I play, for example, my conduct as a teacher or as a husband. The *spiritual me* is the innermost empirical self, the me I hold in the highest regard and about which self-feelings (complacency and dissatisfaction) are most acutely felt and in defense of which self-seeking is most urgently pursued.

In answering the question "What is the spiritual self?" James makes one of his most outstanding contributions. The spiritual me, James considers to be "man's inner or subjective being, his psychic faculties or dispositions, taken concretely, not the bare principle of personal unity or the 'pure ego.' "[31] The spiritual me refers to what is intimate and permanent about myself, the "real" me. We have access to this me when we think of ourselves as thinkers or when we reflect on ourselves as acting. The self here revealed seems to be the active element in our personal consciousnesses, "the source of effort and attention, and the place from which appear to emanate the fiats of the will."[32] The spiritual me seems to be the root of our personality, the source of our interests.

How exactly is this spiritual me experienced; how is it felt? When James describes what the innermost self feels like to him, he confesses he cannot detect the activity of any spiritual process but only bodily movements about the head. He offers these suggestions: when we remember, we feel as if we withdraw from the world. This feeling of withdrawal is caused by the rolling outwards and upwards of the eyeballs. When we consent or negate, the bodily process is the open-

ing or closing of the glottis. When we exert effort, we contract the jaw and chest muscles, "The 'self of selves,' when
carefully examined, is found to consist mainly of the collection of peculiar motions in the head or between the head
and throat."[33] James' claims is not that this is all the spiritual
self is—but that it seems that the spiritual self is *experienced*
as as "collection of cephalic movements of 'adjustment.' "[34]

According to James then, the empirical me, the self as
known, is constituted by various mes which are distinguish-
able by the feelings and actions each promotes. What is the
source of this desire to appropriate—what is self-love? James
argues that self-love is not a mysterious force which impels
us to seek various things; rather, self-love or "my feeling" is
a function of interests. Our consciousness is not merely
cognitional; it is impulsive and interested. The things I
desire are the things that interest me—these interests are
given structures in our natures:

> The sphere of what shall be considered me and mine,
> are but results of the fact that certain things appeal to
> primitive and instinctive impulses of our nature . . . self-
> love is but a name for our insensibility to all but this one
> set of things (which interests us).[35]

For James then, the source of self-love (and the empirical me)
is a given structure of interests in man's nature. Even though
he notes that an explication of these interests is a matter for
ethical and religious philosophy, he gives the following
preview of his analysis. Man's moral and religious experience can be explained in terms of the establishment of a
hierarchy of the various empirical mes and their self-loves.
This hierarchy would be arranged in the light of an ideal
social self who would merit the recognition of God:

[that ideal social self] is at least *worthy* of approving recognition by the highest *possible* judging companion, if such a companion there be. This self is the true, the intimate, the ultimate, the permanent, me which I seek. This judge is God, the Absolute Mind, the "Great Companion."[36]

In our chapter on James' religious and ethical philosophy we will return to this quotation. It is important however to notice that James is indeed writing his psychology with an eye to the "whole man." Here, for example, the demands of the ethical and religious experience are operative in his theory of the empirical me.

We turn now to the other aspect of personal existence, the I, the *self as knower*, the pure ego. The *I* is what is conscious, whereas the me is only one of the things which it is conscious *of*. We have seen that James argues that the spiritual me is *felt* as a complex of cephalic movements; still, we are wont to feel that behind these cephalic movements there is an I, the thinker. James asks what this thinker might be: a state of consciousness, passing thought, a permanent substance, a soul, a transcendental ego or a spirit?

We have already seen James' critique of Hume and Kant —they were not empirical enough in determining their starting point. Hume began with atomistic sensations which were given unity by laws of association. Kant found it unacceptable that these atomic sensations fuse *themselves* together, consequently, he argued the need of a transcendental ego who, as a bystander, would unify the givens of sensation. Thus the task for James is to show the *given unity of passing thought* in order to undercut both positions.

Our ideas are not combinations of smaller atomic ideas. The taste of lemonade is not the taste of lemon plus the taste of sugar. If this were the case, the ideas of lemon and sugar could not fuse themselves, and we would have need of a bystander (ego) which would combine them. Our ideas of a-pack-of-cards-on-the-table is not a composite of the ideas: "cards," "pack," "table," "table legs"; our idea is a single deliverance of the complex thing a-pack-of-cards-on-the-table. James writes:

> The simplest thing, therefore, if we are to assume the existence of the stream of consciousness at all, would be to suppose that things that are known together are known in a single pulse of the stream.[37]

It seems then that the soul is not necessary (at least for psychology) to explain how *knowing* can be accomplished; passing thoughts are sufficient and there seems to be no need to posit a soul as a combining medium. If we grant the *unity of the pulses* of the stream of consciousness, we gain no additional understanding of the knowing process by saying that passing thoughts are acts of a permanent soul.

There is however another argument for the transcendental ego—it can account for personal identity. Thoughts "do not fly about loose, but seem each to belong to some one thinker and not to another."[38] Some of our thoughts have a warmth and intimacy about them and consequently the *me* of yesterday is judged to be the same as the I who now makes the judgment. How do I make this judgment of sameness, for obviously in many ways I am not the same as I was yesterday. James argues that this judgment of sameness is no different than any other—one judges an object the same on the grounds of essential resemblances or the experience of continuity. The me of yesterday is judged the same as the I of now because it is similar and continuous with the I of now. But is it not necessary that there be a permanent abiding principle (an ego) to make this judgment? We need this self-same thinker only if we are not willing to admit the reality of passing states of consciousness. But passing states of consciousness are empirically given.

Even granting the reality and unity of passing states of consciousness, we yearn for a principle of substantial identity. The facts however only require us to suppose a functional identity. Yesterday's thoughts are dead and gone; in there place we have today's thoughts. All that psychology as a science need suppose is passing states of consciousness:

> Successive thinkers, numerically distinct, but all aware of the same past in the same way, form an adequate vehicle for all the experiences of personal unity and sameness which we actually have.[39]

James concludes that all we need suppose for personal identity is a succession of thinkers, each aware of the past in the same way. But how does the I (now, "passing thought") know the past; how can successive thinkers appropriate the past mes? The me I experience now is given with a certain "warmth and intimacy." The past me (of yesterday) is also felt with warmth and intimacy not because I make it mine but because it is mine; it had warmth and intimacy when it was experienced. James uses the analogy of brands on cattle. The cattle bear a brand just as each past *me* bears "warmth and intimacy." But just as the cattle do not belong to X because they are branded; they are branded because they are his. Likewise "warmth and intimacy" do not make the past mes mine; they have warmth and intimacy because they *are* mine. (The past mes are similar and continuous with the I who now judges, and if we lose either feeling of continuity or resemblance, we lose this sense of personal identity.) There is not need of an owner, the bystander ego, because the past mes do not have to be made mine; they were always owned. The present thought is not substantially or transcendentally identical with the former owner of the past self, it merely inherits its "title" and constantly appropriates the past mes:

> It is a patent fact of consciousness that a transmission like this actually occurs. Each pulse of cognitive consciousness, each Thought, dies away and is replaced by another, the other, among the things that it knows, knows its own predecessor, and finding it "warm" . . . greets it saying: "Thou art mine, and part of the same self as me." Each later thought, knowing and including thus the thoughts which went before, as the final receptacle—and appropriating them is the final owner—of all that they contain and own. . . . Who owns the last self owns the self before the last, for what possesses the possessor possesses the possessed.[40]

All that is necessary to account for knowing and the verifiable feature of personal identity is passing thought. As we noted earlier, the positing of a substantial soul would be the path of least resistance given man's religious and moral aspirations, but James' faithfulness to the data of introspection would not permit him to posit such a soul.

We began this third section of our chapter on James' psychology by indicating that his theory of consciousness is central to his interactionist view of man. He argued that introspection reveals thought-going-on and that this thought is personal. Hence an examination of the first characteristic of the stream of consciousness issues in his theory of self. He distinguishes within the stream of personal thought two aspects: the self as known (me) and the self as knower (I). He suggests that successive thinkers who remember what

went before and know what they knew, are sufficient to constitute the *I* as knower. These successive thinkers emphasize
and care for certain aspects of the past thinkers as *me*, and
also appropriate to this me things beneficial to its interests,
e.g., "mine." The innermost center of the me (the spiritual
me) is felt as certain cephalic movements of adjustment. An
aggregate of appropriated things constitute the social and
material me. The I which knows is not an aggregate but passing thought which knows and appropriates the contents of
past thoughts. James argues that he began with what was
empirically given—passing thought, and using it alone he
has been able to account for both knowing and personal
identity.

Bentley[41] and Dewey[42] have argued that James has, in
fact, denied the existence of the self as thinker. They suggest
that James whittled down the subject (I) to passing thought
and reduced the spiritual me to cephalic movements of
adjustment, so that there would be no loss in substituting
for the self, "the ongoing course of experienced things."[43]
Dewey argues that James has written a psychology of phenomenal behaviorism in which the self (I and me) can be
identified with an organism interacting with the environment. Dewey cites as further evidence of James' incipient
biological behaviorism the latter's 1904 article "Does 'Consciousness' Exist?"[44] Undeniably these strains exist in the
Principles, especially in the sections treating the cephalic
movements as biological adjustments. However, James himself does not deny the existence of the I, the thinker. James'
concern is to avoid the separation of the act of consciousness (I) from its content, which is *experienced* in terms of
biological adjustment. The thinker is not a timeless, transcendental ego but thought in a given time and place. James
repudiates both the transcendental ego and the soul for
neither is experienced nor required to explain knowing and

personal identity. Nonetheless he does not go so far as to equate thought with a series of behavioral adjustments. In a word, the precise, pragmatic affect of the demands of the "whole man" in James' psychology is now clear. These demands function to deliniate a parameter within which faithfulness to what is empirically given will be observed. As we have noted, these self-imposed restraints force him, on one hand, to reject the soul as a principle of personal identity, and, on the other, allow him to accept passing thought as the thinker. Hence, James is content to provisionally accept passing thought as the I, the thinker; for the existence of the I is required by man's moral and religious experiences. In turn, he also provisionally accepts an interactionist view of man. Both his theory of man and passing thought as thinker remain provisional positions until he writes the metaphysics of *A Pluralistic Universe*; in both cases his earlier tentative stances are not abandoned but justified.

Since James' theory of the self has touched upon the next three characteristics we will proceed more rapidly. The reader should bear in mind that the importance of these characteristics is not so much in the specifying of James' psychological theory of man as it is in the providing of the ground work for his mature epistemology and metaphysics.

Consciousness is constantly changing

We never experience the same idea, feeling or thought twice, e.g., "no state 'of consciousness' once gone can ever recur and be identical with what it was before."[45] James observes that everyone will admit that we think, remember, hear, feel; but the Lockian school argues that these complex states are only different combinations of simple, unchanging sensations. James suggests that our ordinary experience and language leads us astray, for our interest in the same thing leads us to suppose that the sensations which assure us of this sameness, are the same. We *say* the same taste, same smell but what really is the same is the same *object*.

Our ability to experience the same sensation is notoriously dependent on what we experience immediately before and after a sensation. And also James points out the effect of our mood, age, fatigue, etc. The effect of context and feeling on sensation is explainable by brain physiology. The reason we can never experience an identical sensation is that each sensation corresponds to some cerebral action. If an identical sensation is to recur, it would have to recur a second time in an unmodified brain. But even the first sensation has modified the brain; an unmodified brain is impossible, hence an identical sensation is impossible. "Experience is remoulding us every moment, and our mental reaction on every given thing is really a resultant of our experience of the whole world up to that date."[46] If permanent, identical, atomic sensations are physiologically impossible the next characteristic seems to follow.

Consciousness is sensibly continuous

James characterizes "continuous" that which is experienced without break or division. We have already seen two objections to the unity of consciousness. First, although there may be interruptions or time-gaps (e.g., sleep) in my consciousness, I still nevertheless, experience the "I" of now as the same as the "me" of last night. The self retains *felt* continuity because of the "warmth and intimacy" with which it welcomes the past mes. The second instance of discontinuity in consciousness is the feeling of "breaks" in the quality or content of thought. We are aware of the halting sections of the stream of consciousness (e.g., chair, table, red, cold) but what of the states in between? We have already seen James' objections to Hume and Kant on the *unity of thought*; in this section James details this analysis by investigating both the halting places of consciousness (substantive parts) and the transitive sections (transitive states).

Since the substantive parts of consciousness are more readily observable and correspond to *discrete nameable things*, psychologists have overlooked the transitive parts. James argues they ought just as readily admit the reality of the *feelings* "by," "if," "and" as they admit the reality of the feelings of "blue" and "cold." *Relations* as well as *things* are experienced in the stream of consciousness. James gives several other illustrations of these "felt relations." Notice the differing mental attitudes when someone says "Wait," "Look," "Stop" or the intensively active feeling of "gap" when we try to recall a name and reject candidates which do not fit this unnameable, felt gap. The felt relations which surround the words we use provide their context and may give them a different meaning than they normally have. We are aware of certain expectations of the way a sentence will end and our judgment of the appropriateness of the words that follow is based on a felt relation, which we call rationality. James concludes that the stream of consciousness is continuous:

> The transition between the thought of one object and the thought of another is no more a break in the *thought* than a joint in a bamboo is a break in the wood. It is part of the *consciousness* as much as the joint is a part of the bamboo.[47]

Although we are not often aware of the transitive parts, reflection and analysis will show that they are not only experienced but that as "felt relations" they give meaning and direction to the stream as they conduct us from one substantive part to the next. The fourth characteristic of consciousness has been implied in the above.

Consciousness deals with objects independent of itself

The way consciousness deals with reality is by thought and feeling. James is careful not to degrade the emotive access to subjective feeling or conversely to elevate thought to an objective deliverance. James regards the subjective-objective distinction as a structural-functional contrast of aspects. From a structural point of view, all mental facts are subjective, but from a functional point of view they are objective. The opposition between feeling and thought is false for: "From a cognitive point of view, all mental facts are intellections. From the subjective point of view, all are feelings."[48] Both feeling and thought are cognitive (i.e., about the world) yet the deliverances of each suggest the following distinction to James: feelings yield "acquaintance-knowledge" and thoughts yield "knowledge-about." Our basic access to reality is knowledge by acquaintance:

All elementary natures of the world, its highest genera, the simple qualities of matter and mind, together with the relations which subsist between them, must either not be known at all, or known in this dumb way of acquaintance without knowledge-about.[49]

A blind man may know the physics of color theory but since he does not have acquaintance with color, he does not know color; he only knows *about* it. Through feeling we become acquainted with the world and then by thought we learn about it.

Knowledge by acquaintance is our basic access not only because it is our original relation to the world but because all knowledge must refer back to it. Thus when a psychologist wants to know whether he is dealing with cognitive states (rather than purely subjective states), he uses the practical tests we all use. Our knowledge is about the world if it leads up to, implies, or terminates in our experience of the world, i.e., our acquaintance with the world. Is the world I experience real? This is also practically decided: I experience sameness in a multiplicity of appearances, others concur, and thus the world demonstrates its independence from us.

The theory of knowing sketched here contains the basics of his pragmatism to be treated in our fourth chapter; suffice it for now to add two more points about consciousness as dealing with things other than itself. First, thought need not be conscious of itself to be cognitive of the other, "thought may, but need not, in knowing, discriminate between its object and itself."[50] And secondly, as was noted above, the *object* of the thought "there is a pack of cards on the table" is what is meant by the *whole* phrase, though obviously the topic of the stream of thought, as it proceeds in time, will shift from one idea or felt relation to the next. Only the fifth characteristic of the stream of thought remains.

Consciousness is selective

James considers the selectivity of consciousness to be its most distinctive feature:

> The study of the phenomena of consciousness which we shall make throughout the rest of this book [the *Principles*] will show us that consciousness is at all times primarily a *selecting agency*.[51]

James also states:

> There is one thing which it [consciousness] does, *sua sponte*, and which seems an original peculiarity of its

own; and that is, always to choose out of the manifold of experiences present to it at any given time some one for particular accentuation and to ignore the rest.[52]

Since James' analysis of the mechanism of consciousness's selectivity provides us with the central concept in his interactionist theory of man, we will devote the remaining section of this chapter to this fifth characteristic of consciousness. Before going into this, we should draw together the various strands of James' discussion of the nature of consciousness.

James begins his psychological study of man by indicating that he will adopt an interactionist view of man because its concept of consciousness as efficacious is able to accommodate the desires and interests of the whole man. Despite this overt presupposition, James proposes that psychology be an empirical science, e.g., faithful to the data of introspection. Introspection reveals that thoughts and feelings (he uses the general term "consciousness") are going on. Hence the stream of conscious thought is *continuous* yet ever *changing*. James' analysis of the continuous and changing character of consciousness is not pursued in his psychology (it later becomes crucial for his epistemology), save for his mention that psychologists have only been attentive to the fact that *consciousness deals with objects independent of itself*. These psychologists have overlooked the transitive parts of consciousness (the feelings of relation which reveal the changing and continuous characters of consciousness) and have only noticed the substantive parts of consciousness (which reveal things). James regards the two remaining characteristics as central. He argues that consciousness's dealing with objects independent of itself is not a passive revelation of the world; rather, consciousness actively *selects* for presentation certain aspects of the world because consciousness is *personal*, i.e., responsive to the interests of the knower. Faithful to the data of introspection James is careful to only provisionally accept the existence of the self (I, as thinker) as "passing thought." Notice that James' provisional acceptance of the I as thinker is grounded in the empirically given selective character of consciousness. It is to that characteristic we now turn.

THE SELECTIVITY OF CONSCIOUSNESS ACCORDING TO INTERESTS

James now gets specific about the efficacy of consciousness. He holds that the data of introspection reveal that consciousness is efficacious not by causing ("inwardly creating"); rather, conscious states influence behavior and guide activity by selecting from what is present to it. James will argue that the mechanism of selection is *attention* and that *interests* (practical, aesthetical, ethical, and religious) control consciousness's selective attention. Of special interest in this section is James' analysis of the mechanism of attention and the effect of man's practical interests. While the efficacity of consciousness is most obvious in volitional effort, James argues that consciousness's selectivity (and hence its efficacity) ranges over all conscious states. James examines: sensation and perception of things; belief; conception and reasoning; emotion; instinct; and finally, voluntary action. This order suggests James' adherence to the classical psychological scheme of going from the simple states of consciousness to their compounds—the higher, complex states. Actually what James wants to emphasize is the action of environment upon an organism and its reaction. James begins with the peripheral stimulus, proceeds to the central nervous system, and ends with the organism's response.

Sensation and perception of things

James begins by noting that sensation can only be defined correlatively with perception. Both states are cognitive (i.e., about the world); they are not different sorts of mental facts. The nearer our awareness approaches simple qualities like "hot," "cold," "red," "pain" the more we approach "pure sensation." Conversely, the more we are aware of an object's relation (e.g., its class, location, function) the closer we approach perception. From an analytic point of view sensation "differs from perception only in the extreme simplicity of its content."[53]

Because we can only think or talk *about* what we have directly encountered, we feel forced to posit primitive, pure sensations by which we first were aware of bare natures. Historically, the problem with postulating pure sensations is that these sensations were conceived as static, atomic simples *which were not yet knowledge*.[54] By arguing that sensations are already knowledge, James undercuts the problem of fusing immutable sensations into higher mental functions by postulating a knower to combine and elevate these sensations to the level of knowledge. James distinguishes within knowledge two kinds: knowledge by acquaintance (sensation) and knowledge-about (perception). Thus our first awareness of the world is sensational acquaintance-knowledge of the universe. Gradually we discriminate different aspects of this universe and see relations among them (knowledge-about).

Is it merely frequency that accounts for our discriminating some aspects of our universe, while ignoring the rest? James argues that in particular the British Empiricists have stressed frequency while utterly ignoring "the glaring fact that subjective interest may, by laying its weighty index-finger on particular items of experience, so accent them as to give the least frequent associations far more power to shape our thought than the most frequent ones possess."[55] In short, James contends that we perceive the things we attend to and we attend to the things which interest us.

What is attention? James says he can only describe it as a focalization or concentration of our consciousness. Physiologically, it involves two processes: an accommodation or adjustment of the sensory organs and ideational preparation. The *sensorial adjustment* is easily seen. It can be squinting the eyes, turning the head, etc., when attending a sensible thing or cephalic movements (described above in the experience of activity of the spiritual me) when attending intellectually. *Ideational preparation* is obvious in intellectual attention; likewise in sensory attention we prepare ourselves by the creation of an imaginary duplicate of the object anticipated. For example, when we are told to notice a feature completely foreign to us, we must be told what it "looks like" before we can see it. In fact,

> The only things we commonly see are those which we preperceive and the only things we preperceive are those which have been labeled for us, and the labels stamped on our mind.[56]

Thus we have the elements of perception: the passivity of what is given in sensation and the activity of the mind in attention. Perception is then a combination of "sensational and reproductive brain processes."[57]

In the *perception of things*, consciousness is selective in two ways. First, we choose a group of sensible qualities as signs of the thing. The sensible qualities, "since they are most constant, interesting or practically important, we regard as the essential constituents of the thing."[58] Secondly, consciousness selects which of these qualities (shape, color, sound, size) represent the thing truly or typically. For example, although the retinal sensation given may be two obtuse and two acute angles, we do not perceive a rhomboid table; we see a square one. The table is considered to be square and the other aspects it yields are said to be appearances, modified by the conditions of the moment. A brick presents many shades of red but the one chosen as typical is the one we see in a medium light from close range. The real sound of a cannon is the one we hear when we are close to it. An empty tooth socket feels immense to our tongue yet it is believed to be smaller than a fingertip. A pen held at arm's length covers a book; next to the eye, it covers the whole desk. The correct size in either example is determined according to interests:

> Out of all the visual magnitudes of each known object we have selected one as the *real* one to think of and degraded all the others to serve as its signs. This "real" magnitude is determined by aesthetic and practical interests. It is that which we get when the object is at the distance most propitious for exact visual discrimination of its details.[59]

In all these cases of typical or true representation of the object, we are led quite naturally by experience to choose certain presentations as true and the rest as signs. This is no mystery; the normal position for perceiving things simply offers the most practical advantages. This stress on man's practical orientation provides ample indication of the extent to which James' psychology anticipates his mature epistemological pragmatism.

We never (in adult life) experience pure, uninterrupted sensations; instead we *interpret* the sensations and perceive the most definite and probable thing which past experience has associated with this sensation.[60] If what was presented was X but we perceived Y, we experienced an illusion. However, both illusion and true perception are interpretations. The error in the illusion comes from the mind's contribution. James discusses two ways this may occur. First, we associate what is given with the most probable experience, e.g., when we are in a train and see the train next to us move backwards away from us, we feel as if we are moving forward since our entire field of vision moves backward over our retina (i.e., the same sensation we experience when we move forward). A second type of illusion occurs when the mind is so filled with a certain expectation, any sensation associated with what is expected gives us a sense that the object is really there, e.g., a deer hunter shoots at what he sees to be a deer only to find he has killed a cow; or, when reading one unconsciously corrects a misprinted word.

To summarize, James' previous position that our cognitive access to the world is not a passive reflection but that it is an active selection, is instantiated in his analysis of sensation and perception of things. He has argued that in our perception of things, consciousness selects certain presentations as true or typical (e.g., the true red of a brick is the color presented in medium light, seen at close range). He defined perception as: "part of what we perceive comes through our senses from the object before us, another part (and it may be the larger part) always comes out of our own head."[61] Although the contribution of the mind is always present, it is not a contribution by addition, but a contribution by selective attention to what was presented. What controls consciousness's propensity to attend to certain aspects and to ignore the rest? James suggests that the representations selected as true are the ones most beneficial to our immediate practical needs, e.g., the typical presentations prove to be the most useful to us. Our attention to these typical (e.g., practical and useful) presentations is so habitual that philosophers have assumed that "experience" is the sole determinant of the world which we perceive. James' analysis of the perception of things has shown how incessantly practical interests determine not only *how* we perceive things but that our interests determine *what* we shall experience.

However, we experience many different worlds and each of them is real according to practical, aesthetic, ethical, or religious interests. Hence our next topic: the perception of reality.

Perception of reality: belief[62]

To perceive or experience a thing as real is to *believe* in it. James notes two approaches to this psychical state: what does it consist in and under what circumstances do we adopt this attitude? From the former approach we are only able to say that belief is like an emotion. Its opposite is not doubt but inquiry, and it issues in activity as soon as intellectual repose is accomplished by the cessation of theoretical agitation.

The latter approach is more fruitful. In general, we believe our perceptions reveal the nature of reality and we are prepared to act in ways dictated by those beliefs. However should an experience surprise us and thereby contradict our belief, we become doubtful. Subsequently, we inquire in an attempt to decide between our prior belief and the confounding experience. James contends that since we believe in several different "worlds" (he enumerates seven ranging from common sense to sheer madness) no single criterion for choosing between rival belief claims can be formulated. At this point we will examine only James' account of the common sense world; his analysis of several other types of beliefs will be postponed until our chapter on religious belief.

Why is the common sense world given the prerogative position? Why is this world preeminently *reality* for us? In this world objects not only appear but they appear interesting and important to us. The objects here touch our active and emotional needs. Hence, calling an object *real* adds nothing save reference to us. James considers our cognitive access to the world to be affective; not neutral and objective:

> as thinkers with emotional reaction, we give what seems *to us* a still higher degree of reality to whatever things we select and emphasize and turn to with *a will*.[63]

He suggests that our active, emotional self is the ultimate determinant of our belief in the reality of things. The objects which awaken an attitude of belief in us attach to our subjective interests, be they the pressing practical interests of pleasure and pain or the higher interests: aesthetic, ethical, and religious. He concludes, "our requirements in the way of reality terminate in our own acts and emotions, our own pleasures and pains. These are the ultimate fixities from which the whole chain of our beliefs depend . . . until . . . the supporting branch, the self, is reached and held."[64] In James' view, the source of our sense of reality rests in our interests ("certain postulates given in our nature"),[65] whatever satisfies these interests is believed in as real.

In short, James holds that our belief in any level of reality is directly related to the interests which control our selection of that reality. Not only the interests of the "whole man" (our ethical and religious desires) control our belief (see our next chapter), but even our belief in the common sense world is controlled by interests. The objects we take cognizance of and believe in, as real, in the common sense world are objects which touch our biological needs, i.e., our practical interests.

As we now turn to the distinctive human activities of conception and reasoning, recall the organic framework within which James considers the various forms of consciousness. He proposes that his study of consciousness begins with the environment's action upon the organism and then proceeds to the organism's reaction. However, the human organism does not automatically respond to its environment but a middle stage of mediation intervenes. In this middle stage conception and reasoning occur. Here again James finds confirmation of his thesis that all consciousness is selective—"selection is the very keel on which our mental ship is built."[66] In this discussion James will argue that reasoning is possible by the selective action involved in conception. He suggests that our conceptions select not only according to practical or aesthetic interests but that these selections are further specified in relation to definite purposes.

Conception and reasoning

Reasoning, properly speaking, is not the mere association of a particular experience with another identical or similar experience—James terms this "brute intelligence" or "empirical thinking."[67] Instead, reasoning, by conceiving common abstracted characteristics, is able to handle novelty.

In conception, a part of the whole is selected as essential and in turn, is substituted for the whole. This attribute has meaning only in relation to the concern of the reasoner at that moment and the inferences made by way of those implications are only valid with respect to that concern. This first stage of reasoning is conception and "all the ways of conceiving a concrete fact, if they are true ways at all, are equally true ways. There is no property absolutely essential to any one thing."[68] When we conceive anything we select one attribute and neglect the rest:

> Whichever one of these aspects of its being I temporarily class it under, makes me unjust to the other aspects. But as I always am classing it under one aspect or

another, I am always unjust, always partial, always exclusive. My excuse is necessity—the necessity which my finite and practical nature lays upon me.[69]

In answer to the charge that this view of essence violates the common sense view that a thing's essence makes it what it is, James argues that the mind is essentially a teleological instrument which acts on the basis of interests. What we deem essential properties are only the ones most important to us and our practical (or aesthetic) interests. For example, when I am writing, paper is essentially a surface for inscription. When I need to start a fire it is essentially a combustible thing. Any of the ways of conceiving it are temporary, inadequate and betray the effects of our purposes:

Reality overflows these purposes at every pore. Our usual purpose with it, our commonest title for it, and the properties which this title suggests, have in reality nothing sacramental. *They characterize us more than they characterize things.*[70]

The so-called "essential properties" of things are no more essential or true than the ones we neglect; they are only the more important, more practical, more serviceable properties *for us*. How do we choose which attributes shall be essential? Consciousness, positing certain ends, attends naturally to whatever attributes satisfy these interests. If it is a case of ordinary reasoning, in response to needs, our practical and aesthetic interests direct us to the essential attributes. If it is a case of theoretical thinking, experience, interest, and a curiosity for similarities are operative in consciousness's selection. For example, Darwin's interest and experience allowed him to make the discrimination in the similarity between "rivalry for food in nature and the rivalry

in man's selection (a similarity) too recondite to have occurred to any but acceptional minds."[71] In theoretical thinking, we must notice more subtle likenesses or differences
between objects. To aid in our discrimination between such
attributes, we rapidly shift our attention from one object
to another, and we accumulate many instances of the phenomenon in order to discover differences or similarities
according to the *law of varying concomitants*. For example, if
all wet things were cold and all cold things wet, we would
not likely discriminate between wet and cold. In all thinking,
interest and experience control our discrimination of an
aspect; in theoretical thinking, a curiosity which notices
similarities according to the law of varying concomitants also
aids our discrimination of the correct attribute.

　　To summarize, James' contention that man is "a creature
with partial purposes and private ends"[72] (and that the mind
is a teleological instrument) is borne out in his analysis of
reasoning and conception. He has argued that man reasons
for the sake of action and for the satisfaction of interests.
Further, in the crucial step of reasoning, conception, the
selection of an essential attribute is made in view of a specific purpose. This analysis adds considerable detail to James'
thesis that consciousness is efficacious by way of selection.
Previous to this, James has repeatedly stated that consciousness's selection is controlled by interests, be they practical,
ethical, religious, etc. His analysis of conception (and its role
in reasoning) has shown that he is able to further specify
his contention that interests control selection and that these
interests are "certain postulates given in our nature,"[73] e.g.,
our practical interests control our perception of *paper* as
something useful. Now he has indicated that *within* these
given structures of human nature, he can specify human
purposes, e.g., paper can be conceived of as useful for
writing or useful for burning. James' specification of pur-

poses within the framework of interests gives us a first concrete indication of his theory of humanism: What we choose as essential properties, "characterize *us* more than they characterize the thing."[74]

Having now considered the organism's consciousness of its environment and the mediation of conception and reasoning, we turn now to the organism's reaction. James holds that every conscious state produces a change in the whole organism—" a [conscious] process set up anywhere in the centers reverberates everywhere, and in some way or other affects the organism throughout, making its activities greater or less."[75] Our remaining three sections will consider three kinds of reaction consequent upon conscious states: emotion, instinct, and voluntary action.

Emotion

The two primary responses of an organism's consciousness of an object are inward bodily commotion and direct action. The former is emotion, the latter instinct. The ordinary account of emotion holds that the perception of an object excites a mental affection called emotion and this state of mind gives rise to bodily expression. However, James argues[76] that the reverse order is true—a bodily expression follows directly upon a perception and the *awareness* of the bodily expression is the emotion, his hypotheses states:

> one mental state is not immediately induced by the other, that the bodily manifestation must first be interposed between, and that the more rational statement is that we feel sorry because we cry, angry because we strike, afraid because we tremble and not that we cry, strike or tremble because we are sorry, or fearful.[77]

James' position is not that bodily expression is contributory to emotion, but rather that the awareness of bodily expression is *constitutive* of the emotion—"Bodily changes follow directly the perception of the exciting fact, and our feeling of the same changes, as they occur *is* the emotion."[78] James' contention rests on two points: first, that every perception induces a bodily response and secondly, that each of these bodily changes, however slight it may be, is felt as it occurs. A perception without these bodily changes (and the awareness of the same) is possible, but not for the human embodied consciousness.

James' theory of the emotions constitutes an uncompromising commitment to a psychosomatic psychology—"If our hypothesis is true, it makes us realize more deeply than ever before how much our mental life is knit up with our corporeal frame, in the strictest sense of the term."[79] Even the subtler emotions (moral and aesthetic) involve bodily expression:

> In all cases of intellectual and moral rapture we find that, unless there be coupled a bodily reverberation of some kind with the mere thought of an object and cognition of its quality; unless we actually laugh at the neatness of the demonstration or witticism; unless we thrill at the case of justice, or tingle at the act of magnanimity; our state of mind can hardly be called emotional at all.[80]

There are no special brain centers for emotion; there are as many emotions and individual reactions to objects as there are varieties of bodily changes consequent upon perception.

The history of the controversial reception of James' theory is too far afield for us. We are interested, however, in the following assessment—James' theory of the emotions is behavioristic, i.e., in his account of emotional reactions, consciousness is *not selective*. This assessment ignores two facts: first, the awareness of bodily reaction (which constitutes emotion) is consequent upon perception and we have already discussed the selectivity, according to interests, involved in perception; second, our emotional reaction to a bear in the woods and a bear caged are manifestly different. We do not react to naked objects but to the whole situation; the realization and assessment of the whole situation involves conscious selection.

Instinct

Instinct, or outward action, is the organism's second kind of basic response. The ordinary view of instinct is that it is "the faculty of acting in such a way as to produce certain ends, without foresight of the ends and without previous education in the performance."[81] The account continues by distinguishing the blind and impulsive acts of animals from the rational acts of man. James, analyzing instinct physiologically, begins by saying that instincts are basically reflex actions: man does not lack these impulsive reactions, rather he has them more abundantly. At first glance, James' analysis of instinct appears to be behavioristic; the opposite is true.

Although instincts are reflex actions they are neither blind nor invariable. They are not blind—"every instinctive act, in an animal with memory, must cease to be 'blind' after being once repeated."[82] Instincts are not invariable since experience may substitute one reaction for another or a conflicting impulse may inhibit the original reaction. The more experience molds an organism and the greater the number of conflicting impulses it possesses, the more it seems "to lead a life of hesitation and choice, and intellectual life; not however because he has not instincts, rather because he has so many they block each other's path."[83] James proposes that the nonuniformity of instincts can be explained by the interaction of habit and reflex action. First, habit may inhibit new impulses. An organism becomes so partial to the first specimen of a class that it will not afterward react to others of that class. For example, "the original impulse which got us wives, homes, dietaries, and friends at all, seems to exhaust itself in its first achievements and to leave no surplus energy for reacting on new cases."[84] Secondly, instincts are transitory, and if they are not presented with appropriate objects they will fade away.[85] A child's impulse to nurse soon disappears when it is taught to use a cup even though it would normally continue to nurse for a year. With this discussion of an organism's primary, reflex adjustments to environment as a background, we proceed to the secondary kind of reaction: voluntary action.

Voluntary action

James' concern for the questions of the will and freedom spanned the period from his reading Renouvier's *Essais de Critique Général* in 1879 to his articles in *Essays in Radical Empiricism* (1909). His psychological treatment of the will alone covers some 300 pages, so our treatment can scarcely more than outline his general theory and follow our theme of the selectivity of consciousness. There are two stages in James' treatment of volition, a physiological account of muscular effort and a psychological account of psychic effort, or willing. James' treatment of muscular effort begins with a discussion of the prerequisites for voluntary action.

A voluntary action must be foreseen, hence it follows that voluntary actions are secondary to our primary, instinctive involuntary actions. We must first learn by experience which actions we are capable of: "a supply of ideas of the various movements that are possible left in the memory by experiences of their *involuntary* performance is thus the first prerequisite of the voluntary life."[86] Is anything other than an *idea* (of movement) necessary for voluntary action? Don't we need an idea plus a discharge from a motor center to motor nerves to initiate a voluntary act? For example, the traditional psychological explanation relies on a special nervous discharge going out from the brain to the appropriate muscles. James argues against the existence of this efferent feeling of innervation both from an a priori and an empirical standpoint. A priori the principle of parsimony in psychology urges that consciousness desert all processes where it is no longer useful. An efferent nervous discharge after a motor idea is an unnecessary complication:

> A sharply conceived ideal will directly awaken a distinct movement as easily as it will awaken a distinct feeling of innervation. . . . Whoever says that in raising his arm he is ignorant of how many muscles he contracts, in what order of sequence, and in what degree of intensity, expressively avows a colossal amount of unconsciousness of the process of motor discharge. *Each separate muscle at any rate can not have its distinct feeling of innervation.*[87]

Perhaps then the efferent feeling is a general innervation, e.g., the efferent discharge of effort when we prepare to lift a heavy box. James answers that an empirical investigation shows that what we take to be an efferent discharge is an anticipatory image of the movement's sensible effects, i.e., "afferent sensations coming from the tense muscles, the strained ligaments, squeezed joints, fixed chest, closed glottis, contracted brow, clenched jaw, etc."[88] The reason we are surprised when we go to lift an iron ball and find it to be wooden is because we receive a sensation other than what we expected. Hence from a priori and empirical reasons James denies the existence of efferent feelings of innervation. All that is necessary for voluntary movement is an ideo-motor idea.

James' account of *psychic effort* uses the following example: we know we ought to get out of the warm bed into a cold room but we can't face the uncomfortable consequences so we remain, wanting to get up but not succeeding. Why has this motor idea not initiated a voluntary movement? James answers that the movement would come about save the presence of an inhibiting idea. When we finally get up, "the cold room" did not win over "the warm bed," rather we began thinking about the duties of the day and we found ourselves already getting up: "at that lucky instant the idea (of getting up) awakens no contradictory or paralyzing suggestions, and consequently produces immediately its appropriate motor effects."[89] Hence the general principle can be formulated that every motor idea produces some bodily movement and in the absence of an inhibiting idea, it produces the bodily movement intended. Do we not have to add something dynamic to the ideo-motor idea? James argues that it alone is sufficient, for consciousness is impulsive:

> It is the essence of all consciousness to instigate movement of some sort. . . . Movement is the natural, immediate effect of feeling irrespective of what the quality of feeling may be. It is so in reflex action, it is so in emotional expression, it is so in the voluntary life.[90]

James' account of voluntary action follows his general explanation of instinct and emotion—every idea evokes a bodily expression and conversely every bodily expression evokes a feeling. Our indecision about getting up or staying in bed is resolved when we momentarily forget about the cold floor, and immediately we find ourselves getting up.

James uses this example, particularly the momentary forget-
ting, to analyze the psychic effort involved in voluntary action
following deliberation.

When we deliberate between *A* and *B*, we bring forth the
motives or reasons to settle our indecision. These motives
and reasons reinforce or inhibit our motor ideas. James proposes that since either course of action (*A* or *B*) will take
place whenever the inhibiting ideas are suppressed, willing
consists in *the achievement of the stable presence of an idea:*
"Volition is a psychic or moral fact, pure and simple, and
is absolutely completed when the stable state of an idea is
there."[91] Once the idea is fixed in the mind, the motor consequences follow naturally. Our indecision ceases when we
will the acceptance of the motor consequences of an idea;
psychic effort is the holding fast to an idea (by attention)
and the acceptance of it as real for me. Willing is an affair of
ideas, "volition is primarily not a relation between our self
and extramental matter, but between our self and our own
states of mind."[92] Since the moral action of willing is only
the sustaining of a representation of some action, the resistance we feel in moral decision is only the resistance we have
to an idea and its consequences for us.

In summary, in James' account voluntary action is but
another example of the selectivity of consciousness. Since
ideas will yield their motor consequences if they are not
inhibited by contradictory ideas, willing is not accomplished
by initiating a special current of energy, but by the selection
of ideas by attention. When we attend to an idea (thereby
suppressing its inhibiting contradictory idea), it achieves a
stable presence in our mind and we consent to its reality.
At that moment the task of willing is complete and the motor
consequences follow naturally since ideas automatically evoke
a bodily expression. The effort of willing consists in resolute
attention to an idea; and the feeling of psychic effort is only

consent to the reality of the motor (and other) consequences of the idea.[93]

This concludes our treatment of James' psychology. Even though James originally proposes that psychology be an empirical, ("metaphysically neutral") scientific study of man, his conviction that psychology study the "whole man" leads him to adopt, at the outset, an interactionist view of man in which consciousness is efficacious. He then turns to the data of introspection to see if this view of man will be confirmed. He suggests that two of the characteristics of consciousness— that it is personal and that it is selective, support the efficacy of consciousness, hence this interactionist view of man. Since introspection's deliverance that consciousness is personal only amounts to personal "passing thought," James questions the existence of a substantial soul as source of this personal, passing thought. Obviously the existence of a substantial soul would be most congenial to man's moral and religious experience. James argues that since passing thought can *functionally* account for both knowing and personal identity (which supposedly required a substantial soul) he feels he is only warranted in assuming the existence of "passing thought" as the thinker, as the self, the *I*.

At this point, the philosophy of man exhibited in James' psychology looks very meager—a provisional acceptance of an interactionist view of man and a theory of self in which the I, the thinker, is reduced to passing thought, is also provisionally accepted. Although neither of these stands is finally adjudicated until he writes the metaphysics of *A Pluralistic Universe*, these issues remain central questions in James' philosophy, thus rendering plausible our thesis that James' theory of man provides the proper theme for understanding and unifying his thought.

His analysis of the selectivity of consciousness, however, does both support his interactionist view of man and adds considerable detail to that theory. He argues that in man, mind and body interact by way of the efficacity of consciousness. The mechanism of selection is attention in the stream of consciousness. Further, there is a definite structure of interests in man's nature which controls consciousness's selection. James' repeated reference to the "whole man" is an allusion to the structure of aesthetic, practical, ethical, and religious desires and interests of man. In his psychology, James has analyzed man's practical interests (e.g., his discussion of the practical interests which govern man's belief in the common sense world), and he has shown that these practical interests can be further specified in terms of man's purposes (e.g., his analysis of consciousness's selection of essential properties in conception).

In a word, in his psychology we find James provisionally accepting an interactionist view of man in which consciousness is efficacious. Although the data of introspection, he feels, warrant only a provisional acceptance of the existence of the self as thinker (as the agent of selection) he concludes that the selectivity of consciousness (by the mechanism of attention, controlled by interests and purposes) does confirm the efficacity of consciousness, hence, an interactionist view of man.

Our next chapter will examine the development of James' philosophy of man in his ethical and religious thought. James, building upon the findings of his psychology, turns to an examination of man's religious and ethical experience. He will argue that a study of the desires and interests of the "whole man" confirms his general thesis that consciousness is efficacious (hence, involves an interactionist view of man). Moreover, an analysis of man's ethical and religious interests (and the control they exert in consciousness's selection) will provide added detail to his general theory of man.

3

"Man" in James' ethical and religious thought

In his psychology, James opted for an interactionist view of man since he felt it could accommodate the experiences of the "whole man." The specific experiences of the "whole man" of chief concern to James are ethical and religious; accordingly this chapter will consider: *"Man" in James' ethical thought*, and *"Man" in James' religious thought*. Our efforts in each section will be directed toward determining whether or not his analysis of the experiences of the "whole man" will support and detail his previous commitment to an interactionist view of man; and whether or not his psychological description of consciousness's efficacy—"interested selection"—will be able to account for these experiences.

In his ethical thought, James reaffirms his psychological explanation of choice as consciousness's interested selection. Further, he argues that man's moral experience of responsibility requires that these choices be *free*; in turn, this experience of freedom implies that human actions introduce novelty into the world.

61

In his religious thought, James suggests that since religious experiences occur within a belief-state, an appreciation of these experiences requires an analysis of belief. He will argue that belief is another instance of the selectivity of consciousness and that the desires and interests of man's passional nature control his belief. In his examination of religious experiences, he concludes that although these experiences can be accounted for psychologically, a proper evaluation of them requires an expansion of the notion "human."

"MAN" IN JAMES' ETHICAL THOUGHT: "THE ESSENTIALS OF AN ETHICAL UNIVERSE"[1]

A glance at the philosophical development of James reveals the following: his first philosophical breakthrough was on an ethical question—free will; his early, published works were articles on faith and morals; his first book, *The Principles of Psychology*, concerns itself, in part, with the question of the origin and nature of ethical ideals; and James' own pragmatism is profoundly ethically and humanistically orientated.

Despite all of this James' specifically ethical writings consisted of two articles, "The Dilemma of Determinism" (1884), and "The Moral Philosopher and the Moral Life" (1891).[2] In these two articles, he discusses the possibility of moral experience and two related questions. He begins with a Kantian consideration, "If man's moral experience (especially the experience of responsibly choosing) is genuine, what must be the case?" He then investigates the origin and nature of moral ideals and finally he turns to the resolution of moral conflicts. Our discussion of James' ethical thought will treat these three questions, which he calls, respectively, the metaphysical, psychological, and casuistic questions of ethics.

Although James' discussion of these three questions obviously does not constitute an ethical system, it does contribute to his theory of man. His conclusion to the metaphysical question—man is free—supports his interactionist view of man in which consciousness is efficacious by selection and his discussion of the second two questions explicates how ethical desires and interests (specified by moral ideals) control consciousness's selection.

Metaphysical question—possibility of moral experience

James begins his ethical investigations by asking what are the conditions of the possibility of moral experience. The moral experience he considers paradigmatic is man's experience of *responsibility for action*. He concludes that three conditions are requisite: that man possess true freedom, that man's free acts introduce novelty into the world, and that the world be ongoing and unfinished.

James' first philosophical breakthrough came in 1870. He felt oppressed and helpless in the face of his father's Calvinism with its predestination doctrine. Reading Renouvier's *Essais de Critique Général* helped him counter the feeling of impotence and opened for him a possible justification of free will. James' diary for April 30, 1870, reads:

I think that yesterday was a crisis in my life. I finished the first part of Renouvier's second *Essais* and see no reason why his definition of free will "the sustaining of a thought *because I choose to* when I might have other thoughts"—need be the definition of an illusion. At any rate, I will assume for the present . . . that it is no illusion. My first act of free will shall be to believe in free will.[3]

It is evident that this insight, "sustaining a thought because I choose to," provided the core of his psychological account of volition. James' stream of consciousness theory holds that free will and the consequent feeling of effort be explained in terms of *attention*. Each mental representation in the stream of consciousness automatically evokes a bodily response (consciously or unconsciously felt), and our freedom consists in our "selective attention" to mental representation A rather than the conflicting representation B. When we hold before our mind, long enough, the representation A (instead of B) the self (mind and body) responds with an appropriate action. James makes it clear that he wants "to emphasize the fact that volition is primarily a relation between, not our self and extramental matter, but between our self and our own states of mind."[4] This relation between the self and its own states of mind involves the following:

> The operation of free effort, if it existed could only be to hold some ideal object or part of an object, a little longer or a little more intensely before the mind. Amongst the alternatives which present themselves as *genuine possibles*, it would thus make one effective.[5]

Thus James holds that his stream of consciousness theory, utilizing the mechanism of selective attention is able to offer a psychologically sound explanation for free will.

On the question of free will, James, the psychologist, is officially neutral; but James, the ethician and metaphysician, is a passionate defender of freedom. James' main philosophical works (especially *Pragmatism*, 1907, *A Pluralistic Universe*, 1909, and *Essays in Radical Empiricism*, 1912) are metaphysical justifications of freedom. His most striking justification of free will, however, is his essay "The Dilemma of Determinism." He argues that in order that man's moral experience of responsibility be possible, man must possess *true freedom*, that is, man's free acts must introduce novelty into the world, and hence determine the future of an undetermined world.

As the title suggests, James' task is to show the incongruities of determinism. He begins by showing that there is no pragmatic difference between the "hard" determinists who speak of fatality and predetermination and "soft" determinists who, à la Spinoza, refer to freedom as necessity understood. The real issue is between determinism and indeterminism. The alternatives are not freedom as a function of ignorance *or* freedom as necessity understood but predetermination *or* novelty. Determinism professes:

> That those parts of the universe already laid down absolutely appoint and decree what the other parts shall be. The future has no ambiguous possibilities hidden in its womb: the part we call the present is compatible with only one totality.[6]

In a determined world only one future is permissible and that future has been fixed eternally by the past. Indeterminism, on the contrary, holds that there are real possibilities in the universe; real novelty and radical becoming are possible: "The parts of the universe have a certain amount of loose play on one another so that the laying down of one of them does not necessarily determine what the others shall be."[7] In this world, since the past does not absolutely decree the future, the true originality of free actions is possible. The metaphysical structure of the two worlds is starkly different. Determinism's world is a "block universe" and the sole categories of the real are necessity and impossibility. True freedom in the determined world can only be an appearance. Indeterminism's world is unfinished, ongoing, and it can accommodate novelty, for genuine possibilities are real.[8]

The central message of the article concerns the pragmatic

difference between determinism and indeterminism, namely, that determinism can neither make sense of nor support *moral experience*. James gains access to the possibility of moral experience by an analysis of "judgments of regret" in a deterministic world. Let us suppose that there has been a senseless, cruel murder and we react by expressing regret that such a thing has happened.

> The judgment of regret calls the murder bad. Calling a thing bad means, if it means anything at all, that the thing ought not to be, that something else ought to be in its stead. Determinism, in denying that anything else can be in its stead, virtually defines the universe as a place in which what *ought to be* is impossible.[9]

In a determined world, the murder was necessary—the murder was consistent with the whole universe, since it was predetermined by the events before it. Hence, regret for murder turns into regret for the whole world and we are at the doorstep of Schopenhauer's pessimism. We may however exchange our pessimism for deterministic optimism by holding that what appeared to be bad was really good if looked at from the right perspective. If we should choose to adopt a systematic optimism, we ought to abandon our judgments of regret (at a particular occurrence and at the whole world). But abandoning our judgments of regret leads to a curious logical predicament. If we are optimists, our judgments of regret are wrong. Yet if the world is determined not only the "evil" act but also our original judgment was determined. If we are optimists the murder was really good, i.e., not regrettable; nevertheless, our initial wrong judgment was determined. In a determined world regrets are "theoretical absurdities and errors."[10] On the other hand, if the original judgment was right then the "evil" act was truly evil. But both the act and our judgment were determined; hence the dilemma of determinism:

> Murder and treachery cannot be good without regret being bad; regret cannot be good without treachery and murder being bad. Both, however, are supposed to have been foredoomed; so something must be fatally unreasonable, absurd and wrong in the world. It must be a place of which either sin or error forms a necessary part.[11]

There is something fundamentally unreasonable about a world in which there must be necessary evil or necessarily erroneous judgments. In the face of a determined world, our attempt at optimism turns into pessimism, for in this world "good and bad," "regret and approval," are meaningless, moral striving is an absurd activity and we, at last, abandon ourselves to an inactive fatalism. No effort is worthwhile and life is a *vanitas vanitatum*.

Indeterminism's world is drastically different—because being fragile and open to the effects of moral action, it can support moral experience:

> I cannot understand willingness to act, no matter how we feel, without the belief that acts are really good and bad. I cannot understand the belief that an act is bad, without regret at its happening. I cannot understand regret without the admission of real, genuine possibility in the world.[12]

If our experience of free will is to make sense and if we are responsible for the world our actions create, the world must be unfinished, liable to be injured or enhanced by our free choices. If the world is unfinished and restless, our actions make a difference. James' view of the world is neither optimistic nor pessimistic—it is melioristic. The world may become better or worse, it depends on the exercise of our free will.

Recall that in his psychology James opted for a view of man which could support the experiences of the "whole man." In this ethical investigation he has analyzed one of these experiences. Man experiences not only that his thoughts and feelings direct his behavior (this much was argued for in James' interactionist view of man in which consciousness is efficacious by selection), but that he is responsible for his behavior. James has argued that the possibility of this moral experience of responsibility requires that man possess *true freedom* (as opposed to freedom as a function of ignorance or freedom as "necessity understood"), that man's free acts introduce novelty into the world, and that since man's free acts introduce novelty into the world, the world be undetermined.

James' view of man now includes not only an interactionist view, but that man is free and that man's free acts determine the future of the world by the introduction of novelty. James has also argued that the empirically given selectivity of consciousness can psychologically account both for man's experience of directing his behavior and his moral experience of the volitional effort attendant to his responsibly choosing. Man's moral choices are made in light of ideals and to these we now turn.

Psychological question—origin and nature of moral ideals

In his psychology, James argued that the interests which control consciousness's selection are *structures given in human nature*. He now attempts to refine this claim by giving a more detailed account of the nature and origin of the structures which control moral choices—moral ideals.

Psychologists, attempting to discover the origin of moral ideals have adopted one of two alternatives, evolution or intuition.[13] James begins with an appraisal of both accounts.

The evolutionists have contended that "good" and "bad" are simply remote associations with either beneficial, pleasurable experiences or harmful, painful experiences. James agrees that this is a plausible account for some of our values, but it fails to explain many of our higher ideals which are not simply functions of association with sense impressions nor mere feelings of utility.

The opposite attempt at explaining the origin of our moral ideals is offered by the intuitionists. They hold that most of our ideals are sentiments of "felt fitness" which have little or nothing to do with habit or utility. The intuitionists hold that,

all the higher, more penetrating ideals are revolutionary. They present themselves far less in the guise of effects of past experience than in that of probable causes of future experience, factors to which the environment and the lessons it has so far taught us, must learn to bend.[14]

This account argues that our ideals are a priori structures in human nature.

James concludes that neither the evolutionists' nor the intuitionists' explanation is satisfactory. However, both have something to offer. Our moral ideals are neither simply given a priori nor are they simply long-past associations of pleasure and pain. James then refers us to his own attempt to combine both accounts—the last chapter of his *Principles of Psychology*, "Necessary Truths and the Effects of Experience."

Our specific question comes up in the context of his treatment of the larger question of the experiential origin of necessary propositions. He treats the propositions of the pure sciences (logic and mathematics) and argues that the propositions (ideals) of aesthetic and ethical systems are of the same type. The question is then—what is the origin of necessary propositions, and ethical and aesthetical ideals? Once again we meet the opposing camps: evolutionists and intuitionists. James points out that both agree that the elementary qualities (e.g., cold, hot, pleasure, pain, red, blue, sound, etc.) are "original, innate or *a priori* properties of our subjective natures even though they should require the touch of experience to awaken them."[15] The empiricists hold that all combinations of these elements are dependent upon sense experience, while the intuitionists hold that some forms of combination are possible apart from sense experience.

James first treats the empiricists. Their claim is that all the connections among ideas in the mind are fruits of the pressure of the world given in sense impressions. They hold that we deem a proposition necessary because it has always been so experienced. James counters that we deem propositions necessary not because of experience but because of the meanings we have attached to the words. Experience can neither yield nor overthrow necessary propositions:

> How could our notion that one and one are eternally and necessarily two ever maintain itself in a world where every time we add one drop of water to another we get not two but one again . . . at most we could then say (according to experience) that one and one are *usually* two.[16]

Necessary propositions are about the meanings of words: "Logic, classification, and mathematics all result from the mere play of the mind comparing its conceptions, no matter whence the latter may have come."[17] Nevertheless, the intuitionists' account is not totally satisfactory, for obviously experience has some role to play in our awareness of word-meanings and hence necessary propositions. James' explanation for the effect of experience upon necessary truths (and ethical and aesthetical ideals) is a combination of the two positions.

He begins by distinguishing two kinds of experience: "front-door" and "back-door." "Front-door experiences" are experiences of adaption. In these experiences, by association and habit we learn how to respond to environment. Our experience of a fire is associated with pain and we learn the correct adaptive behavior—"don't get too close."

The second type of experiences is the "back-door" variety. Here the reaction of the mind is not a semi-automatic adaptive response to environment. In this case a perception leads to another mental attitude—our perception of a camp fire, for example, may not wake any response associated with survival or comfort; instead we may be struck by its beauty. The "back-door experience" which leads us to think in terms of beauty rather than adaptive behavior is not explainable by "front-door experience." That a fire should stir thoughts of beauty cannot be explained by association or habit—it is a "brain-born experience."

> Our higher aesthetic, moral and intellectual life seems made up of affections of this collateral and incidental sort, which have entered the mind by the back stairs, as it were, or rather have not entered the mind at all but got surreptitiously born in the house.[18]

Hence James contends that many of our moral ideals are derived (by "back-door experience") from a priori structures in our nature. However, "front-door" experience also affects our moral ideals, for our moral ideals cannot be completely divorced from the world we live in. Moral ideals might indeed be "back-door and brain-born" but they must be attuned to the world and responsive to "front-door experience." Ideals must be acted upon if they are to be meaningful. To be acted upon, they must be translatable into adaptive behavior (which is learned by "front-door experience").

James argues then that moral ideals arise from the effect of "front-door" and "back-door" experiences on a priori, elementary mental structures:

> The moral principles which our mental structure engenders are quite as little explicable *in toto* by habitual experiences having bred inner cohesions. Rightness is not *mere* usualness, wrongness nor *mere* oddity, however numerous the facts which might be invoked to prove such identity. Nor are the moral judgments those most invariably and emphatically impressed on us by public opinion. The most characteristically and peculiarly moral judgments that a man is ever called on to make are in unprecedented cases and lonely emergencies, where no popular rhetorical maxims can avail, and the hidden oracle alone can speak; and it speaks often in favor of conduct quite unusual, and suicidal as far as gaining popular approbation goes.[19]

Even though some of our moral ideals are derived by associations of pleasure and utility ("front-door" experience), James considers that the paradigmatic moral ideals are the result of "back-door" experiences, operating on the a priori structures of the mind. He describes the interplay between "back-door" experiences and the given structures in the mind as follows:

the forces which conspire to this resultant are subtle harmonies and discords between the elementary ideas which form the data of the case. Some of these harmonies, no doubt, have to do with habit; but in respect to most of them our sensibility must assuredly be a phenomenon of super-numerary order, correlated with a brain-function quite as secondary as that which takes cognizance of the diverse excellence of elaborate musical compositions. No more than the higher musical sensibility can the higher moral sensibility be accounted for by the frequency with which outer relations have cohered.[20]

James maintains that the following examples show that mere frequency (of past associations) could not have generated these paradigmatic moral ideals:

Take judgments of justice or equity, for example. Instinctively, one judges everything differently, according as it pertains to one's self or to some one else. Empirically one notices that everybody else does the same. But little by little there dawns in one the judgment "nothing can be right for me which would not be right for another similarly placed"; or "the fulfillment of my desires is intrinsically no more imperative than that of anyone else's"; or "what it is reasonable that another should do for me, it is also reasonable that I should do for him"; and forthwith the whole mass of the habitual gets overturned. It gets *seriously* overturned only by a few fanatical heads. But its overturning is due to a back-door and not a front-door process.[21]

His account of the origin of moral ideals, then, consists in a critique of both the habitual association and the a priori structural accounts. James opts for a combination of both accounts: although ideals are derived from "back-door" experience working on the a priori structures of the mind, they must feel the corrective pressure of "front-door" experience (associations of pleasure and pain) else they will not guide behavior. While we can quite readily agree with James' critique of the intuitionists and the evolutionists, his own solution adds little illumination.

Although James' account of the origin and nature of moral ideals proves unsatisfactory, it indicates his own dissatisfaction with the somewhat simplistic position in the *Principles*, namely, that the desires and interests which control consciousness's selection (here, the ideals which control consciousness's selection in moral choices) are simply given structures in man's nature. If moral ideals were given structures, one would expect easy and frequent unanimity in moral matters. The exact opposite is closer to the truth. James attempts to account for these individual differences in ethical attitude and conduct in terms each man's unique experience (of both varieties) molding the given structures of his nature. Obviously, if each man's moral ideals are uniquely individual and if each man made moral decisions only in terms of his own moral ideals, his actions would likely conflict with the moral ideals of his neighbor or the moral code of society. James attempts a resolution of these conflicting moral hierarchies in his discussion of his third question of moral philosophy—the casuistic question.

Casuistic question—society, religion, and the individual

James discusses the problem of competing value hierarchies in terms of the de facto individual-society dialectic. Although a final resolution of the dialectic seems unlikely, he suggests that religious experience may offer a solution.

That there are ethical conflicts surprises no one. James

notes that in these conflicts, even an appeal to the authority of a divine thinker and his ideal moral hierarchy only postpones the problem. "Truth cannot be a self proclaiming set of laws or an abstract 'moral reason,' but can only exist in acts or in the shape of an opinion held by some thinker really to be found."[22] However, we cannot simply accept each person's ideals as the law-giving ones.

Can an impartial test of competing ideals be found? Many have been suggested—the good is: the mean between extremes, what makes man happy, what brings perfection and dignity, what harms no one and benefits most, etc. But there are conflicts among these impartial tests and "after all, in seeking for a *universal* principle we inevitably are carried onward to the most universal principle—*the essence of the good is simply to satisfy demand.*"[23] Instead of offering a new impartial test, James suggests the following. The quest for an absolutely impartial test of ethical ideals ought never have occurred. We err if we desire to be impartial in matters of ethics, for ethics and ethical ideals only have meaning when we are not disinterested spectators but involved actors. We do not encounter the world as a disinterested spectator for we go to the world with our temperament, our education and our social background. We can only look at the world as a "selective interpreter." To use John Dewey's analogy, we never encounter raw material but we only experience refined metal.[24] Rather than despair at our inability to see things disinterestedly and "objectively" we need only examine the de facto ethical dialectic between the individual and his society.

The demand for subordination of moral hierarchies is not a theoretical one for the detached philosopher; it is a pressing practical need. Subordination of ideals can only be done at the concrete level and the ethical experiment on this concrete level is already in progress. "We are blinded to the real difficulty of the philosopher's task by the fact that we are born into a society whose ideals are largely ordered already."[25] Society is an historical experiment in satisfying as many ethical demands as is possible, "those ideals must be written highest which *prevail at the least cost*, or by whose realization the least possible number of other ideals are destroyed."[26] The society we are members of has shaken itself into a balance, satisfying the maximum number of needs. James, then, seems to resolve the question of competing moral hierarchies by holding that society's mores and laws embody an adequate moral hierarchy. Actually nothing would be more alien to the spirit of James' thought.

To gain the full impact of James' views on ethical subordination we must utilize his distinction of "front- and back-door" experience. The dialectic between the ideal and the real is largely between "back-door" and "front-door" experiences. Since most ideals are derived from "back-door" experience, there will always be the gap between the ideal and the real, between the "ought" and the "is." But, as was mentioned earlier, ideals cannot be too ideal or they hold no sway in our conduct. "Front-door" experiences must adjust the "back-door" derived ideals or they become meaningless.

James draws an analogy between ethics and science. In both there is a gap between "front-door" experience (fact, reality) and "back-door" experience (theory, ideal). In science, the gap between fact and theory is pragmatically dissipated by the process of verification. If a scientific theory ("back-door" derived, for theories are more the result of selective interpretation than a simple compilation of data) cannot predict a sensible effect (observed by "front-door" experience) the theory is modified or abandoned. Science, then, has a built-in system of aligning theory and fact.

In ethics there is the same sort of gap, this time between the ideal and reality. The pragmatic experiment to adjust the ideal and the real is undertaken by society. It seems part of human nature that most of the aligning would be in favor of downgrading the ideal to fit the real. Unfortunately, this is only too true. But there is also present in man the opposing desire to change the real, uplifting it to the ideal. Thus there are in man two moods: a *genial mood* which lowers ideals to fit the real and a *strenuous mood* which strains to lift the real to the ideal.

The prevalent force in society is generally a conservative, genial mood which adjusts the ideal to the real in much the same way as the process of verification in science adjusts the theory to the facts. However, the real impact of a moral ideal is to uplift the real to the ideal. The ethically sensitive person is of the strenuous mood; he is the change-oriented individual in society. For James, the paradigm ethical act occurs when one man opposes the conservative mood of society and stands up to be counted. James' paradigm ethical act is of the type exhibited in John F. Kennedy's *Profiles in Courage.*[27] James states:

> The most characteristically and peculiarly moral judgments that a man is ever called on to make are in unprecedented cases and lonely emergencies, where no popular maxims can avail, and the hidden oracle alone can speak; and it speaks often in favor of conduct quite unusual, and suicidal as far as gaining popular approbation goes.[28]

For James, the true meaning of a moral ideal is most obvious when a single man rises to challenge the status quo.

There are two difficulties at this point: what will urge a man to adopt a strenuous mood; and we seem to have gained no ground on the problem of conflicting value hierarchies, for while society's experiment promotes the genial mood, paradigmatic moral judgments urge the individual to challenge society. James suggests that we look to religion and sainthood, respectively, for the solution of these two problems.

How is the strenuous mood awakened? James feels that a Marxian type appeal to work for the future of humanity will not work because we can't love future men. James posits that the only adequate stimulus to the strenuous mood is moral companionship with God. God opens the infinite perspective and "the more imperative ideals now began to speak out with altogether new objectivity and significance and to utter the penetrating, shattering, tragically challenging note of appeal."[29] A commitment to God will help the individual to abandon the genial mood of prudence and satisfaction of merely finite and personal needs and take upon himself the strenuous tasks. Belief in God increases our moral energy and gives us the desire to take the uncomfortable path.

How can religious experience help remove the relativism from the paradigm moral judgments (those of the strenuous mood, made apart from and often in opposition to society)? James' answer is that in fact history has shown that the most satisfactory moral hierarchies (and consequently the most perfectly moral, human lives) have been the fruits of man's religious experiences. In James' Gifford Lectures, *Varieties of Religious Experience*, we find a lengthy study of mysticism and its moral effect—sainthood. Mystical knowledge is superior to the normal ways of knowing just as the real is superior to the logical—"If the mystical truth that comes to a man proves to be a force that he can live by, what mandate have we of the majority to order him to live in some other way?"[30] The truth that the mystic lives by, produces in him moral excellence—sainthood. Thus, for James, the answer to the conflict between the genial and strenuous moods and the apparent subjectivism of the moral decisions which opt for a change in society, is sainthood:

> It is quite possible to conceive an imaginary society in which there should be no aggressiveness, but only sympathy and fairness,—any small community of true friends now realize such a society. Abstractly considered, such a society on a large scale would be the millennium, for every good thing might be realized with no expense of friction. To such a millennial society the saint would be entirely adapted. . . . The saint is therefore abstractly a higher type of man than the "strong man" because he is adapted to the highest society conceivable, whether that society ever be concretely possible or not.[31]

This utopian rhapsodizing has an essential *theoretical* function in James' ethical thought. Moral ideals need not necessarily conflict and the distinction of the genial and the strenuous moods need not obtain. Theoretically, at least, a single moral hierarchy and its embodiment in a society is possible. The distinctive characteristic of that millennial society would be a perfect fit between the real (society) and the ideal (embodied in the moral excellence of the saint).

James' discussion for the casuistic question of ethics is important for this theory of man for its distinctive Jamesian emphasis of individuality. Although he recognizes society's practical experiment in resolving moral conflicts, he argues that the paradigmatic moral judgments of the strenuous mood spring from the unique sensibilities and temperament of each man. Our appraisal of his suggestion that religious experience may resolve the conflicting moral moods must be deferred until we treat his religious thought. James here, then, re-emphasizes his stand on individuality, and he indicates that he sees as one of the effects of religious experiences that they encourage individuals to follow the moral urgings of their own unique temperament and sensibility.

It remains for us to summarize James' ethical thought with a view to the theory of man it explicates. James began his psychology by opting for a view of man which could accommodate the experiences of the "whole man." His ethical thought investigates one of these experiences: man's moral experience of his responsibility for his actions. In his discussion of the *metaphysical* question of ethics, James argues that man's moral experience requires that man possesses true freedom, man's free acts introduce novelty into the world, and since man's free acts introduce novelty they will determine the future of an undetermined, unfinished world. James' theory of man, hence, includes in addition to an interactionist view of man in which consciousness is efficacious (i.e., man's experience that thoughts and feelings direct his behavior), a commitment to freedom and to the idea that man's free acts introduce novelty into the world's future (i.e., man's moral experience of responsibility for his behavior).

In his discussion of the *psychological* question of ethics, James argued that his psychological explanation that consciousness is efficacious by selection can accommodate man's moral experience of the volitional effort attendant to his responsibly choosing. He then attempted to refine his stand on the nature and origin of ethical desires and interests (moral ideals) which control consciousness's selection in moral choices. He concluded that moral ideals are not simply given structures in man's nature, but they are "sentiments of felt fitness" which are generated by an interplay between given structures in man's nature and "front- and back-door" experiences. Although it remains unclear what these structures are and how experience molds them, it is clear that James is searching for a way to account for the diversity of moral ideals. He argues that the paradigmatic moral judgments occur when an individual heeds the call of his own unique moral sense. This emphasis on individuality is important for it indicates the direction James' theory of man will take—he is as equally interested in individual differences in man as he is in the shared structures which characterize the human way of being.

In his discussion of the *casuistic* question of ethics, James examines society's ongoing attempt to cope with individual differences. Obviously, if each individual responded only to his own moral ideals, conflicts would ensue. This difficulty is specious, argues James, since individuals are in fact born into societies which are already ordered by moral hierarchies. These moral hierarchies are the result of a pragmatic experiment in satisfying as many moral demands as is possible. However, if moral conflicts were always resolved by an alignment of the individual's moral sense with society's existing moral code, the moral judgments which James considers paradigmatic (i.e., an individual in response to his unique sensibilities, rising to challenge the status quo) would never be operative, nor would the uniqueness of individuals ever be expressed. At this point, James turns to religious experience, in order to offer the two following suggestions. First, belief in God gives the individual courage to adopt the strenuous mood instead of living the genial mood. And, second, religious experience produces a distinctive kind of ethical excellence. The ethical excellence of the saint provides us with a pattern for an ideal ethical hierarchy. With this reference to religion in the context of ethics, we turn now to James' religious philosophy, noting how closely religion and ethics are interrelated in

James' mind—religion promotes ethical action and conversely, ethical actions are used to evaluate religious experience.

"MAN" IN THE RELIGIOUS THOUGHT OF JAMES

Religious philosophy is generally primarily concerned with the existence and nature of God and only secondarily with the difference belief in God makes in man's life. However, it is not surprising that James' religious philosophy accentuates the latter and makes only passing reference to the former. His discussion of God and religion is distinctly man-centered; he is concerned with the nature and function of belief in God and the difference that belief makes. In James' view, religious philosophy considers three questions: the nature and legitimacy of belief; the effect of belief; and the existence and nature of the object of belief. James treats the first question in his series of essays published as *The Will to Believe*, the second in *The Varieties of Religious Experience*, and the third in his metaphysical writings, *A Pluralistic Universe* and *Essays in Radical Empiricism*. Since our interest in this chapter is the theory of man developed in James' ethical and religious thought, we will restrict our discussion to the first two questions.

Through an analysis of religious experience, James further elucidates his view of the "whole man." However, since religious experience presumes and works within a belief-state, he first analyzes the nature and legitimacy of belief in general and religious belief in particular. James will argue that the familiar psychological explanation of consciousness's efficacity-selection, can account for the experience of belief, and further, that belief, in all levels of reality, is controlled by the desires and interests of man's passional nature. He then turns to a description and a psychological explanation of the effects of religious belief—religious experiences.

Nature and legitimacy of belief

James' concern with these problems was sustained from his early articles, "The Sentiment of Rationality" (1879), and "Reflex Action and Theism" (1881), to his later essays, "The Psychology of Belief" (1889), and "The Will to Believe" (1896).[32] The first three articles mentioned were discussions of the nature of belief and the last, a treatment of legitimacy of belief. Presuming the context of this theory of the nature of belief, James summarized the legitimacy of belief, his "will to believe" doctrine, as follows:

> Our passional nature not only lawfully may, but must decide an option between propositions, whenever it is a genuine option that cannot by its nature be decided on intellectual grounds; for to say, under such circumstances, "Do not decide, but leave the question open," is itself a passional decision,—just like deciding yes or no,— and is attended with the same risk of losing the truth.[33]

James' defense of the legitimacy of belief was so thoroughly misunderstood that he was charged with justifying belief in whatever one desired and guaranteeing the right to make believe. For example, in a previously unpublished letter to C. S. Peirce, February 3, 1899, James complains:

> I ought to have answered your last letter, relative to my "Will to B[elieve]" about which I have been in much hot water lately. Foolish review of it by Miller in Int[erna-national] J[ournal] of Ethics. Had I instead of that inglori- ous title called it "a critique of pure faith" or something like that, those criticisms would have no ground to stand on. Of course, I admit that a man may defend a cause no longer believed in by himself, out of obstinacy, etc. But I do not consider those cases—they are not fit for

general treatment. No one knows how much perversity may or may not enter into his own beliefs—let alone his neighbors. I had the pragmatic end in view of deciding whether the logical conditions which beset the relations of our passional nature with the truth on one side, and our means of knowing it for certain on the other, were such as to forbid or to legitimate the individual in "trusting his lights" at his own risk. I decided that they legitimated him; and I do think that an important point gained for one's practical attitude toward the religious faiths of the world. They are unavoidable functions of man. I fancy the only original point in the whole essay to have been the emphasis laid on the distinction between the two risks, that of loosing the truth and that of incurring error.[34]

It is our contention that neither James' sympathizers nor his critics have correctly appreciated the larger context of his theory of belief (specifically an account of the procedures of acquiring beliefs) and hence have not properly treated his discussion of the legitimacy of certain types of beliefs. Although this doctrine is admittedly dramatic it is not especially radical when viewed as a particular instance of his general view of man's nature.

1. *Nature of belief.* We have already discussed James' analysis of belief in the common sense world. James described belief as a conscious state akin to emotion, characterized by a willingness to act. For James, the key words in the previous sentence are "emotion" and "act." The things that are deemed real in our common sense world are the things that appeal to our desires and interests; in short, the things we believe in touch our emotional and passional natures. However, belief is not simply *mentally* entertaining as real what

our emotions prompt; belief leads to action. These actions, consequent upon belief, correct our beliefs in terms of successful or abortive interaction with the world. As we turn to the other types of belief (scientific theories, philosophies, and religious beliefs) we will notice that James discovers the basic nature of belief to consist in these two moments: first, our passional nature legislates the selection of which aspects of the world we shall consider real and, second, the actions which belief induces exert a corrective adjustment of those beliefs.

In our belief of scientific theories the corrective pressure of experience is obvious. While not wishing to ignore the pragmatic importance of empirical falsification or verification of a theory, James' concern is to emphasize the effect of our passional nature in our choice of theories. The latter effect is not readily recognized until we must decide between two rival theories which equally well accommodate sensible experience. At this juncture the effect of emotional and aesthetic desires comes to the fore, and a theory is chosen on the basis of simplicity, elegance, etc. James' commenting on a current example—the rival one and two fluid theories of electricity, says:

> That theory will be most generally believed which, besides offering us objects able to account satisfactorily for our sensible experience, also offers those which appeal most urgently to our aesthetic, emotional and active needs.[35]

Although the occasion of choosing between equally satisfactory theories may seldom occur, it points out the often neglected impact of our passional natures.

James discovers the same two factors, the dictates of our passional nature and the pragmatic impact of our actions, controlling our belief in philosophies. In response to a felt need, we philosophize "to attain a conception of the frame of things which shall, on the whole, be more rational than the rather fragmentary and chaotic one which everyone . . . carries about with him."[36] James suggests that we recognize rationality as we recognize anything else—by its subjective effect on us, in this case, a strong feeling of ease and peace.

James contends that we believe a philosophy when it satisfies certain desires thereby bringing a feeling of rest. These desires are both theoretical and practical. He reduces the theoretical demands to two: a desire for simplicity and a desire for clearness:

> No system of philosophy can hope to be universally accepted among men which grossly violates either of the two aesthetic needs of our logical nature, the need for unity and the need for clearness, or entirely subordinates the one to the other.[37]

A theoretically adequate philosophy must both appreciate the individual objects in our world and at the same time unify these particulars by reducing them to a few (or one) explanatory principles. A suitable philosophy must also satisfy our practical nature and its demands. James here finds three basic demands. First, the ultimate explanatory principle "must not be one that essentially baffles and disappoints our dearest desires and most cherished powers."[38] James notes that, for example, Hartmann's basic principle, "the unconscious" confounds us and Schopenhauer's "vicious will-substance" dampens our willingness to act. Second, we not only desire that our powers be stimulated but that our choices and actions be relevant. James here points out that the absolute monism and determinism ignore this demand. And third, our practical nature demands that a philosophy "banish uncertainty from the future"[39] by providing an appropriate guide for action. The choice of a philosophy to be believed in is, at bottom, controlled by our passional nature—a philosophy is accepted and deemed rational when it brings us a feeling of ease. We feel at ease when certain theoretical demands are satisfied and our practical natures made relevant and given suitable guidelines for action.

James suggests that belief in a melioristic philosophy most adequately satisfies man's interests and desires. As we shall see, this particular philosophy displays a peculiarity which lays the groundwork for the will to believe doctrine. If we choose to believe in a melioristic philosophy, not only are our most cherished powers appealed to and made relevant, but the actions this belief promotes actually help produce a melioristic universe. In this case, our actions help to create verification of our belief—"This world is good, we must say since it is what we make it,—and we shall make it good."[40] James here is pointing out the psychological fact that belief in the possibility of a future fact is one of the factors in bringing about the existence of that fact. For example, if I enter into marriage believing that it will be a successful, permanent union, my belief helps make it so. A melioristic philosophy appreciates this fact (besides satisfying the other passional demands):

No philosophy will permanently be deemed rational by all men, which (in addition to meeting logical demands) does not in some degree pretend to determine expectancy and in a still greater degree make a direct appeal to all those powers in our nature which we hold in highest esteem. Faith being one of those powers, will always remain a factor not to be banished from philosophic constructions, the more so since in many ways it brings forth its own verification.[41]

In James' view, a melioristic philosophy is the most rational philosophy for it is aligned with our passional demands (theoretical and practical), and it urges the full use of our powers. In this type of belief, actions consequent upon that belief do not serve to correct the initial belief so much as to actually produce verifications of the belief. James sees a similar situation in religious belief.

James' analysis of religious belief follows the familiar pattern—belief in God is rational for it leaves us with a feeling of ease and it furnishes an adequate stimulus to our practical natures. We feel at home in a situation when we attain a conception which orders and unifies our experience. The situation at issue here is not the meaning of a particular experience but the meaning of the whole universe and our place in it. The mind asks the ultimate "why" and "what" of the universe and the conception the mind forms to answer these questions is God. James holds that when we are faced with the mystery of the whole world and our place in it, we attain a feeling of peace by the conception of God: "God whether he exists or not . . . would form *the most adequate possible object* for minds framed like our own to conceive as lying at the root of the universe."[42] However, since we are primarily creatures of action, our conceptions are not had for their own sake (contemplation) but they are for the sake of action. James lists as support for his claim for the priority of man's active nature his analysis of mind. Our mind, he argues, has a triadic structure wherein perception and conception issue in reaction, e.g., if I am tired of standing and I see a chair, the perception "hard surface" is followed by the conception "it is solid and will support me," which in turn initiates the reaction of my sitting on the chair. By analogy, if our perception of the whole world leads to the conception of God, what will be the proper reaction to this conception? Since God is conceived as the creator of the world who holds certain purposes dear, our

reaction will be moral action—"co-operation with his purposes."[43] In summary, religious belief is rational, since it ful-
fills our theoretical demands by answering the ultimate questions and it makes relevant our practical life (cooperation
with God's purposes). Further, the moral actions religious
belief stimulates help produce verification of the initial belief
in God by making the world more moral and thereby increasing our sense of the presence and purposes of God.

From this analysis of the nature of belief James has
established the following. The only criteria available to us in
acquiring beliefs are (1) the practical and theoretical demands
of our passional nature, and (2) the pragmatic test of experience which corrects our beliefs. Further, (3) in the special
cases of moral and religious beliefs, the actions consequent
upon our belief actually produce their own verification.
Given this analysis of the nature of belief, we now have the
proper context to appreciate the will to believe principle:

> Our passional natures not only lawfully may, but must,
> decide an option between propositions, whenever it is
> genuine option that cannot by its nature be decided on
> intellectual grounds, for to say, in such circumstances,
> "do not decide, but leave the question open," is itself a
> passional decision,—just like deciding yes or no and is
> attended with the same risk of losing the truth.[44]

This statement of James' of the *legitimacy* of belief, affirms
that the decision not to believe without sufficient intellectual
evidence is itself a passional decision and further (and herein
lies James' defense of the right to believe), this passional
decision may prohibit us from gaining the truth. James will
argue that W. K. Clifford's injunction—"It is wrong always,
everywhere and for everyone, to believe anything upon in-
sufficient evidence,"[45] is irrational for it deprives us of the
possibility of truth.

2. *Legitimacy of belief.* James begins his analysis of the legitimacy of religious belief with the larger issue of our duty as knowers. There are two great commandments—"Know the truth" and "Avoid error"; they are materially different duties. Our inclination toward one or the other is based on our passional nature. Since Clifford regarded the risk of error paramount, he exhorts us only to believe in the face of convincing intellectual evidence. James, on the other hand, argues that knowing the truth is our primary duty and in our search for truth "our errors are surely not such awfully solemn things."[46] James however, argues that experience has taught us that when we are not presented with a crucial practical decision, we do well to not make up our minds until we have sufficient evidence.[47] Nonetheless, some critical decisions must be made without the benefit of sufficient evidence. For these decisions James carefully specifies that stringent conditions must be satisified. The decision at issue must be concerning a genuine option which is forced, living and momentous. For example, James considers "Shall I believe in God?" such a critical decision. For a twentieth-century American the option, "Be a theosophist or be a Mohammedan," is dead while, "Be a Christian or an atheist," is a live one. The religious option is obviously momentous for it is embraced as a way of life. Is, however, the religious option forced? It seems not, for we can be a believer, an atheist, or an agnostic. James argues that since religion concerns *actions*, the decision to be an agnostic is equivalent to the decision to be an atheist. In this case, waiting for more evidence amounts to a refusal to act, thereby refusing to produce the facts which could verify the initial belief in God.

> Since belief is measured by action, he who forbids us to believe religion to be true, necessarily also forbids us to act as we should if we believed it to be true. The whole defense of religious faith hinges upon action.[48]

The difference religion makes is a difference in actions; hence the agnostic position prevents action as surely as the aesthetic stand. James argues that in this forced, living, and momentous option, the rational move is to believe without sufficient evidence, else we are deprived of an opportunity to gain truth. In this particular case, belief is legitmate; we have the right to believe.

James' analysis of the nature and legitimacy of belief follows the following line of reasoning. Since he holds that belief is a conscious state, akin to emotion, characterized by a willingness to act, he is not surprised to find that the interests and desires of man's passional nature influence our beliefs. In fact, he contends that we treat as real only that which touches our interests and urges our actions. Our discussion has indicated the effect of our passional natures in several kinds of belief. The second moment of belief, the pragmatic test of experience, was also discovered in the various types of belief. James' position then is that our desires do not simply legislate beliefs but that, beliefs, as practical guides, prompt actions which serve to correct the initial beliefs. Further, in the special case of religious and moral beliefs, James points out a peculiarity: in these cases the effect of the actions dictated by beliefs is to produce verification of the initial beliefs. In these special cases, if we are faced with a living, momentous, and forced option, we have the right to believe without having beforehand sufficient evidence. This is so, argues James, precisely because the decision to withhold belief (itself a "passional decision") deprives us of the chance to gain certain truths made so by our actions.

James' analysis of the nature of belief is a dramatic example of his general theory of man. He holds that human activity is characterized by an exquisite dialectic. Man's emotional and passional nature prompts him to select certain aspects of reality while ignoring others. (James' insight into and analysis of the pervasive selectivity of consciousness is distinctive among American pragmatists.) In the second stage of the dialectic, man acts in accordance with this selection; the success or failure of his actions coerces adjustment of his initial belief concerning the nature of reality. James then investigated the validity of this dialectic apropos of man's moral and religious belief. In these cases he found the first moment of the dialectic unchanged but the second moment altered since the action prompted by religious and moral belief do not correct so much as confirm the initial beliefs. For example, belief in God may produce conversion, an increase in moral vigor, even sainthood and mysticism, and to these effects we now turn.

Effects of religious belief: an examination of the religious propensity in man

In 1901-2, James gave the Gifford Lectures on Natural Religion (at Edinburg); these lectures were published in 1902 as *The Varieties of Religious Experience*. James' original plan called one half of the twenty lectures a description of various religious experiences and the other half a metaphysical analysis of the same. James so extended his descriptive task that the latter consideration was reduced to a single lecture. Accordingly, the volume was subtitled, *A Study in Human Nature*. This subtitle is important for our study of James' thought. Recall that he opted for a view of man which could accommodate the experiences of the "whole man." This subtitle indicates the extent to which *all* experiences are operative in James' theory of man. For James, if a theory of man does not include all recognized sorts of human experiences, it is not a theory of man. He argues in the *Varieties* that religious experiences are not sham, nor are they mysterious, therefore unanalyzable; rather they are human experiences which are amenable to psychological explanations. James' empirical and psychological approach to the varieties of religious experience is intended to allow for an appreciation of the humanness of these experiences. In James' view, a study of religious experience is primarily important for what it tells us about man, not for what it tells us about God. His whole orientation to belief and its effects, religious experiences, is an attempt to widen the notion of *human* experience.

James restricts his subject matter to personal religious experiences, since he regards institutional religions (and the theologies they generate) as secondary fruits of someone's private, germinal religious sentiments and feelings. Hence the subject matter is, "the feelings, acts, and experiences of individual men in their solitude, so far as they apprehend themselves to stand in relation to whatever they may consider the divine."[49] James' procedure is to give a general description of the experience in question (e.g., conversion or sainthood), exhibit a variety of concrete examples (generally taken from autobiographies), draw empirical generalizations, give a tentative psychological explanation, and finally attempt to appraise the significance of the experience in terms of its practical fruits. Since James' aim is an empirical study of religious experience, he exhibits a broad variety of religious experiences, and he refuses to exclude even the most extreme examples. James' attempts at psychological explanation are not to be construed as a Freudian or Feuerbachian reduction of religion to organic disorders or pathological wish fulfillments. Tracing a religious state to its organic or psychic cause does not prejudice its value; instead, it helps us understand that the phenomena of religious experience are additional instances of the psychosomatic condition of man. Further he argues that the religious impulse in man is rooted in very definite needs and desires in man's nature; discovering what these needs and desires are will give us a fuller appreciation of man's nature. James holds that we ought to judge the truth of a religious experience the way we judge the truth of any experience—by its factual evidence, by the consistency of these alleged facts with our accepted beliefs, and by the congruence of this experience with our passional natures. Hence, the criteria for the truth of religious experiences are "immediate luminousness, philosophical reasonableness and moral helpfulness."[50] In short, religious experiences are not to be judged by their origins but they ought to be evaluated experientially in terms of their effects in us.

In the *Varieties*, James analyzes the religious propensity of man as it develops from a primal sentiment to its ultimate form in mysticism. Although we will touch on all the moments of this development, for the sake of clarity we have divided our treatment into four sections: first, the primal religious sentiment; second, conversion—gradual and sudden; third, the effects of conversion: an evaluation of sainthood; and fourth, mysticism and natural theology as warrants for the unseen world.

1. *Primal religious sentiment.*   James begins by arguing that religious sentiment is generated in response to man's wonder about the totality of things and that God is conceived as a being who can answer this basic human yearning. Further, he suggests that whether our initial reaction to God be joy or sadness is dependent on our individual temperament. As was noted above, James holds that our primal religious experience is the feeling or sentiment generated in our reaction to the whole world—"religion, whatever it is, is man's total reaction upon life."[51] Hence, the religious sentiment is characterized, generally, by our reaction to the whole world and, specifically, by our conception of the divine as the source and director of the whole world. This conception of God promotes in us a joyful yet serious attitude that "all is not vanity in this universe, whatever the appearances

may suggest."[52] Because God is conceived as the deepest power in the universe, personally caring for certain purposes and me, the religious sentiment induces an enthusiastic, emotional, active commitment in the place of a stoic resignation to necessity. Whether our initial response to God and the universe be sadness or gladness provides James with a basic distinction of the kinds of religious sentiment.

Our initial response to the universe and God as its creator may be that "God loves me and the world is a good place." James describes this religious optimism as the *religion of healthy mindedness*. These religious optimists feel the world, nature, man, and themselves to be naturally good and beautiful. This feeling of goodness may be involuntary (natural) or voluntary (systematic). The former group, (for example, Walt Whitman, Rousseau, Saint Francis) seem to see nothing but goodness in the world. They seem innocent of the presence of evil. The latter see evil in the world, but their conviction that the world is, at bottom, good, allows them to systematically ignore evil by explaining it away as an appearance. These individuals, (for example, Spinoza, Leibnitz, Bradley) are able to see goodness by attaining a different, divine perspective from which to look at the world. Both kinds of healthy minded individuals see the world as naturally good, and hence they need only be born once to attain religious joy.

A second type of initial reaction to the world and God is characterized by a profound sense of the precariousness of our existence, the ubiquity of evil and the perverseness of our wills. This group James calls the *sick souls*. Since their initial reaction is sadness they must die to this world and be born again to experience religious joy. This initial state of religious melancholy springs from a feeling that something is radically wrong with the world and with man. James gives lengthy, autobiographical examples (Goethe, Luther, Tolstoy) describing how the original optimism and self-satisfaction of each was eroded by a feeling of the vanity of mortal things, a sense of profound sinfulness, or a fear of the whole world. The essential conviction of the sick soul is that the evil in the world cannot be ignored or explained away.[53] The proper remedy for this religious melancholy is religious conversion.

2. *Conversion—gradual and sudden.* For the sick soul to attain happiness, the natural man must die in order that the new spiritual man may live. The sick soul is not unaware of the good in himself and in the world, but he is also acutely conscious of the presence of evil. He possesses a divided self, composed of the natural (consciousness of evil) and the spiritual (awareness of good) man. The process of conversion begins with the struggle between the two selves and is concluded in a reunification characterized by peace, happiness, and insight into religious truth. It is important to notice that the converted sick soul does not become a healthy-minded individual:

> Neither Bunyan nor Tolstoy could become what we have called healthy-minded. They had drunk too deeply of the cup of bitterness ever to forget its taste, and their redemption is into a universe two stories deep. Each of them realized a good which broke the effective edge of his sadness; yet the sadness was preserved as a minor ingredient in the heart of the faith by which it was overcome. . . . Tolstoy does well to talk of it (a new center of energy) as *that by which men live*, for that is exactly what it is; a stimulus, an excitement, a faith, a force that re-infuses the positive willingness to live even in the full presence of the evil perceptions that erewhile made life seem unbearable.[54]

The converted sick soul is no longer unaware of evil, but he is able to live in the face of its reality since he has the energy to work against it. James summarizes his description of conversion as "the process . . . by which a self hitherto divided and consciously wrong, inferior, and unhappy, becomes unified and consciously right, superior and happy, in consequence of its firmer hold upon religious realities."[55] James' psychological account of this reunification of a divided self provides us with one of his most interesting and instructive contributions.

James' account of conversion is an application of his psychological doctrine of the various empirical mes which are contained in the self. We are, in fact, various selves, each with its own group of ideas and interests centered on a particular aim. James gives an example of the president of the United States on a camping trip. He actually becomes a different person since his usual system of purposes and ideas (chief of state) is removed from his attention and in its stead, a new center of interests and desires (backwoods man) governs his attitudes and activities. We all undergo similar minor alterations of character as we act out our different selves, e.g., father, teacher, sportsman. If we should entertain habitually one or another of our various selves, we are transformed and become that self. Religious conversion is an instance of this transformation caused by a shift in attention to a special group of ideas and interests. "To say that a man is 'converted' means, in these terms, that religious ideas, previously peripheral in his consciousness, now take a central place, and that religious aims form the habitual centre of his energy."[56] The converted person's life is now governed by a new system of ideas and these ideas now channel his energies.

How do religious ideas, previously peripheral, move to the center? The candidate for conversion feels his present incompleteness and wrongness (a sense of sin) and, concomitantly, a positive ideal of the kind of life he wishes to live. Although all conversions contain both the above elements, either element may be primary thus establishing two general types of conversion—voluntary ("a process of struggling away from sin") or self-surrender ("a positive striving toward righteousness").[57] Psychologically, these two types are analogous to the common experience of trying to remember a name. We may either recall the name by working for it, mentally clustering all the associates we can summon or if that process proves unsuccessful we may give up the search, think of something else, and suddenly, we have the name. Conversion also occurs in these two ways—a person may struggle against sin and actively strive for conversion or he may give up the struggle and gradually become transformed. In either type of conversion, the desire for a new life has set into motion a process James calls "unconscious celebration" or "subconscious incubation."[58] Religious ideals and desires previously on the periphery of consciousness begin to develop and unify and when they have "ripened" they suddenly burst upon consciousness replacing the old system of ideas with a new center of life. In both types of conversion the moment of rebirth occurs when the person gives up the struggle and surrenders himself to the mercy of the divine. James writes that conversion can be explained by:

> The shifting of men's centres of personal energy within them and the lighting up of new crises of emotion. . . . The phenomenon [is] partly due to the explicitly conscious process of thought and will, but [is] largely also due to the subconscious incubation and maturing of motives deposited by the experiences of life. When ripe, the results hatch out, or burst in to flower.[59]

In James' view, gradual conversion can be psychologically explained by the following. The active longing for a new religious life, along with a conscious striving against sin, activates a subconscious incubation of religious ideas. When these ideas have matured (by forming a new center of personal energy) *and* the person surrenders himself to God (by dying to the old self) conversion occurs when the new religious center of ideas replaces the old.

But what of *sudden conversion*? In these instances there seems to be neither an active struggling nor an unconscious incubation. Here conversion seems so striking and miraculous that a natural explanation seems impossible. Not so, claims James. He begins by noting that religious conversions (gradual or sudden) belong to the general class of phenomena called automatisms (posthypnotic suggestions, automatic writing, unaccountable impulses or inhibitions, obsessive ideas, etc.) in which memories, thoughts and feelings, though unconscious, definitely influence our conscious thought and behavior. James' field of consciousness theory holds that a personality is composed of both conscious and subconscious elements and that a hard and fast boundary cannot be drawn between the two. Hence the eruptions of the subconscious are not miraculous incursions from an undetermined source, rather they are manifestations of the subject's wider personality. James' psychological account of gradual conversions utilized this view of personality—the conscious struggle against the old self generates subconsciously the new self. In the case of sudden conversion, the subject does not require a long period of struggle and subconscious incubation, for he possesses a more active and well developed subconscious self. This type of personality is the paradigm example of the divided self—he possesses both a conscious and a subconscious self. Since this type of person is especially susceptible to suggestions, his moment of rebirth consists in a sudden change of personality wherein the active and well developed subconscious self replaces his conscious self.

In this analysis of conversion, James has shown how a supposedly miraculous event can be amenable to psychological explanation. He has accounted for gradual conversion in terms of a personality change caused when a new structure of ideas and interests replaces the old structure, and hence, controls behavior. James has suggested that yet another human experience, here conversion, can be accounted for by the selectivity of consciousness (here, directing behavior), and that this selectivity is controlled by interests (in this case, religious interests and ideas). His explanation of sudden conversion utilizes the

same framework of a shift in ideas and interests plus the existence of an active, well-developed subconscious self. We shall
see more of this subconscious, wider self in his treatment of
mysticism; now, however, there is a difficulty—James' explanation of the religious experience of conversion seems to have
explained away "religious."

This psychological account of conversion raises two problems: the first is the common objection that a psychological
explanation reduces conversion to a purely natural phenomenon
and second, if in the face of the first objection, the supernatural character of conversion is still maintained, the supernatural–natural chasm is so obliterated that the distinction
between them becomes meaningless. In response to the first
objection, James argues that even if the phenomenon of conversion be amenable to natural explanation (e.g., the presence
of the subconscious self) the possibility of the direct presence
of the divine is not precluded. In fact, the subconscious may
be our access to the higher spiritual agencies:

> Just as our primary wide-awake consciousness throws open
> our senses to the touch of things material, so it is logically
> conceivable that *if there be* higher spiritual agencies that
> can directly touch us, the psychological condition of their
> doing so *might be* our possession of a subconscious region
> which alone should yield access to them.[60]

In any case, whether the origin of conversion be purely
natural or supernatural forces, the value of the forces and the
experience can only be appraised in terms of their fruits, not
their roots:

> Our spiritual judgment, . . . our opinion of the significance
> and value of a human event or condition, must be decided
> on empirical grounds exclusively. If the *fruits for life* of a
> state of conversion are good, we ought to idealize it and

venerate it, even though it be a piece of natural psychology;
if not, we ought to make short work of it, no matter what
supernatural being may have infused it.[61]

Discovering the origin or giving a psychological account of a
religious experience does not prejudice the value of that occurrence. Its value can only be judged on the basis of what it attains
—its practical consequences. In answer to the second objection,
James sees no problem in obliterating the natural-supernatural
chasm. In fact, if there is not a chasm between orders of
human excellence, we have removed the anomaly of the person,
claiming no religious conversion or divine inspiration living a
superior, yet natural, life. If there is to be a difference between
the natural and the supernatural it would be one of degree.
However, the fruits of religious conversion, conspicuous by
their excellence, argue for the supernatural character of conversion. The unusually strong and lasting, even heroic ethical
effects of conversion may issue in a distinct quality in the
believer—sainthood—and to this state we now turn.

3. *Effect of conversion: an evaluation of sainthood.*   The immediate effects of conversion consist in peace and security at feeling
whole along with a feeling of closeness to the divine and a joy
in the goodness of the world and one's fellowmen. The practical consequences of this affective state are a surrender of self to
God and to neighbor. The surrender to God expresses itself in
humility, asceticism, chastity, poverty, and obedience. The
feeling of freedom and joy at the loss of the self produces in the
believer a profound tenderness toward others, issuing in concrete acts of charity. Thus the distinctive characteristic of saintliness is a surrender to God wherein self-interest is replaced by
an active concern for one's neighbor.
    James next turns to an evaluation of the fruits of conversion.
Since the basic effect of sainthood is the dissipation of the self

with its interests and desires (our *immediate* criteria for value judgments) we must look for a more general criterion. James proposes: "to test saintliness by common sense, to use *human standards* to help us decide how far the religious life commends itself as an ideal kind of human activity."[62] In other words, do the fruits of sainthood adapt the possessor to the ideal human society.

At least one group of religious virtues fails to satisfy this criterion. Religious fervor may lead to a fanatical, ascetic, asocial love of God to the exclusion of love of neighbor. The religious fanatic may become so utterly unwordly that the normal human concerns for this life (e.g., temporal welfare, love of family and friends) become regarded as unnecessary, even sinful, distractions. However, if surrender to God issues in a commitment to fellow men, it promotes a better society. In this society, charity and love of fellowman encourage human excellence—respect for the sacredness of all persons and a tolerance of individual differences:

> It is . . . quite possible to conceive an imaginary society in which there should be no aggressiveness, but only sympathy and fairness,—any small community of true friends now realizes such a society. Abstractly considered, such a society on a large scale would be the millenium, for every good thing might be realized there with no expense of friction. To such a millennial society the saint would be entirely adapted. . . . The saint is therefore abstractly a higher type of man than the "strong man," because he is adapted to the highest society conceivable, whether that society ever be concretely possible or not.[63]

In this society, characterized by the celebration of man's highest values, the saint would be perfectly adapted. Unfortunately since this society does not exist, we must attempt an evaluation of sainthood of terms of present society. The saintly virtues (felicity, purity, patience, self-severity, which Nietzsche termed the cowardly, soft virtues) seem to ill-adapt their possessor to present society. However, if everyone possessed the "hard" virtues, their aggressiveness would either destroy society or reduce it to a master/slave caricature of community. Our present society contains a mixture of both the aggressive and the nonviolent virtues and accordingly if adaptation to present society is to be our criterion, the fruits of sainthood would be valuable if they were to exhibit a mix of the soft and hard virtues. But what of the reference to ideal human society, for surely our present society is not ideal?

At this juncture James follows the same tack as he did when treating the impact of morality. The essence of moral ideals is to inspire in man the strenuous mood; moral ideals ought to be the change-orientated, uplifting force in society. The raison d'etre of moral ideals is to urge change and improvement of the status quo, likewise the real impact of religion ought also to be to urge improvement and upgrading in society. James argues that the religious message is compromised if it be reduced to promoting the genial mood; it ought to inspire the strenuous mood: "If religion is true, its fruits are good fruits, even though in this world they should prove uniformly ill-adapted and full of naught but pathos."[64] However, if we wish to retain "environmental adaptation" as our evaluating criterion we must decide whether "the seen world or the unseen world be our chief sphere of adaptation."[65] If we are to consider adaptation to the unseen world, we must examine the religious vision of that world—mysticism.

Before we proceed to James' analysis of mysticism and natural theology, it will be helpful to retrace his reasoning thus far. We began our examination of the *Varieties* by noting that James proposes to analyze religious experiences in order to show that they are human experiences and to expand our notion of "human." So far in his analysis of the primal religious senti- ment, conversion, and sainthood, he seems to have only pur- sued his first objective—i.e., to show these experiences to be human by explaining them psychologically.

This charge arose earlier in the form of the objection that his analysis of conversion explained away the religious nature of that experience. He responded that psychological explanation does not preclude the supernatural character of an experience and that the natural/supernatural distinction is based on a differ- ence of degree, not kind. He suggested, for example, that the ethical excellence of sainthood exemplifies this difference in degree, and hence, its supernatural character. When he attempted a practical evaluation of the virtues of sainthood in terms of environmental adaptation, he concluded that this prac- tical criterion compromised the meaning of that religious experi- ence. In other words, he argued that if the meaning of the reli- gious experience of sainthood is to be properly evaluated, we must not use ordinary human experiences as a criterion; rather we must expand our notion of human experiences. He suggests that sainthood must be evaluated in terms of its experience and vision of the unseen world—i.e., mysticism. We turn now to James' analysis of mysticism and natural theology as warrants for the unseen world. It is crucial to understand that James' interest is not per se in the unseen world, but that our notion of "human" is to be expanded in terms of the reality of the unseen world and its effects on the believer.

4. *Mysticism and natural theology as warrants for the unseen world.* James begins his account of mysticism by giving four distinguishing characteristics of this state of consciousness. First, *ineffability*: "the subject of it immediately says that it defies expression, that no adequate report of its contents can be given in words."[66] Mystical states must be experienced, that is, like

feelings they must be known by acquaintance; knowledge about them will not suffice.[67] Secondly, although mystical states are akin to feelings, they have definite *noetic quality*. Despite the fact that the cognitive content cannot be articulated, a deep, lasting personally authoritative insight into religious mysteries is conveyed. Thirdly, *transcience*; these states are brief, rarely lasting even half an hour. And lastly, mystical states are marked by *passivity*: "The mystic feels as if his own will were in abeyance, and indeed sometimes as if he were grasped and held by a superior power."[68] Although the mystic may follow a well ordered preparatory regimen, the moment of mysticism "happens" to him; he does not cause it.

Although the mystical state be authoritative for the mystic, what warrant of the unseen world does it furnish for the rest of mankind? James offers a three-part answer. First, for the mystic these states are, and have the right to be, absolutely authoritative: "If the mystical truth that comes to a man proves to be a force that he can live by, what mandate have we the majority to order him to live in another way?"[69] Secondly, although the outsider has no duty to accept uncritically the mystic's revelation, the consensus of mystical deliverances ought to constitute a presumption in behalf of the unseen world. However, since it is only a presumption or a suggestion it must be tested along with our other presumptions, i.e., by experience—its fruit for life. Thirdly, "the existence of mystical states absolutely overthrows the pretension of nonmystical states to be the sole and ultimate dictators of what we may believe."[70] James suggests that our ordinary accesses to reality (sense and understanding) are not our only access. Yet even though mystical states may be a superior access to a wider world, the mystical deliverances (of this unseen world) are so various, the nonmystic is once again forced to use the only test at his disposal—experience.

James concludes that although mysticism corroborates the religious vision of the unseen world, its testimony is too private and various to establish an objective warrant for the existence of the unseen world. Even though in his analysis mystical states have failed to prove the existence of the unseen, they have expanded our notion of "human." "Human" will now include the existence of mystical states of consciousness. The existence of this special access, argues James, "absolutely overthrows" the claim that our ordinary experiences are the only access to reality, and finally, the deliverances of mystical states constitute a presumption in favor of the existence of the unseen world and its effects in men's lives. James next turns to another attempt to establish a warrant for the existence of the unseen world—natural theology.

James' treatment of the philosophical attempts to establish a warrant for religious belief is an extended discussion of his earlier claim that theological formulation and argument are secondary products of religion's primary source—private religious sentiment. "These speculations must, it seems to me, be classed as overbeliefs, buildings-out performed by the intellect into directions of which feelings originally supplied the hint."[71] Intellect's work upon the data of faith consists in amplifying, defining, and defending what is already believed. James lists as support of his contention that religious feeling is prior and primary to reason's systematization, the failure of the proofs for the existence of God to engender belief in the nonbeliever. Proofs for God's existence, while convincing to the believer, seem singularly unconvincing to the unbeliever because neither party shares the same initial premise. The theist's premise is a nonrational feeling or intuition that the *whole world* is caused, in short, that the world is created and hence demands God as a creator. This premise is not shared by the atheist. However, reason's attempt to delineate and specify faith are valuable insofar as they serve to enliven and solidify belief; for example, the attempts to delineate the attributes of God. James submits that the delineation of the *metaphysical* attributes of God (aseity, oneness, simplicity, immutability, etc.) arise from a mistaken conception of thinking. James had previously argued that thinking is for the sake of behavior, hence if the metaphysical attributes of God do not make a difference in our conduct they are devoid of intellectual significance. Since these attributes:

> Call for no distinct adaptations of our conduct, what vital difference can it possibly make to a man's religion whether they be true or false.[72]

James here returns to his original contention that the difference religion makes is a difference in the way life is lived. If these attributes of God do not issue in a change in our conduct, they are meaningless. The *moral* attributes of God, however, do define our conduct, hence they constitute a meaningful addition to faith. Believing that God is holy, omnipotent, just, or loving positively determines our fears, hopes, and expectations. In short, our belief in the moral attributes of God, guides our conduct toward God and neighbor. James' account of the role of reason vis à vis religious belief amounts to two claims: since religion is primarily and fundamentally a matter of belief (sentiment), reason cannot engender belief by establishing a warrant for religious experience, and reason's attempt to elucidate the content of belief is only valid insofar as its contributions serve the believer by making a practical difference in his actions. In short, James argues that religious experiences occur within a belief-state and since the factors (the demands of our passional nature) which control this belief are prerational, reason cannot engender belief. He holds that reason works within and subsequent to, a belief-state, hence its role is in defining and enlivening what is already believed.

Recall that James' concern was the possibility that mysticism and natural theology could establish an objective warrant for the unseen world. In turn, our notion of "human" would be extended to include that unseen world thus providing the proper context for evaluating sainthood. Neither mysticism nor natural theology accomplished its task. The question which remains unanswered is, precisely how do religious experiences expand the notion "human" and how is this added dimension to be evaluated? James now attempts a different tack.

He first gives the following summary of the beliefs which are embodied in religious experiences:

1) That the visible world is part of a more spiritual universe from which it draws its chief significance.

2) That union or harmonious relation with that higher universe is our true end.

3) That prayer or inner communication with the spirit thereof—be that spirit "God" or "law"—is a process wherein work is really done, and spiritual energy flows in and produces effects, psychological or material, within the phenomenal world.

Religion, he goes on to say, includes also the following psychological characteristics:

4) A new zest which adds itself like a gift to life, and takes the form either of lyrical enchantment or of appeal to earnestness and heroism.

5) An assurance of safety and a temper of peace and, in relation to others, a preponderance of loving affections.[73]

James' analysis of the variety of religious experiences has shown that these experiences spring from human desires—for example, a concern for individual destiny and for the meaning of the totality of existence. Hence, from the outset James emphasizes that the religious impulse is rooted in needs and desires which are part of man's nature.

If these experiences have as their source human needs and desires, why then must they be evaluated? Cannot they be simply accepted as valid dimensions of the human condition? At this juncture, it is important to recall James' theory of belief. He argued that beliefs are controlled by the desires of our passional nature and they are corrected by experience. However, in religious (and ethical) beliefs, he has suggested, experience does not so much correct our beliefs as help create the verification for these beliefs. James' attempt to evaluate religious experiences (occurring within religious beliefs) is to determine whether or not these experiences attach to anything "in reality" or are the objects of belief simply *created* by our passional needs. James' evaluation begins by distinguishing the effects of religious belief into thoughts and feelings.

The characteristic feeling engendered by religious belief is a "stenic" affection, "an excitement of the cheerful, expansive, dynamogenetic order."[74] The religious faith-state imparts a zest, a joy, a willingness to live. Since religion provides men with a force by which they can live and live happily, at least from the point of view of *subjective utility*, religious feeling must be judged valuable. To pass beyond subjective utility we must turn to the objective, *thought* content of religion.

James holds that the common core of religion's noetic content consists of an account of two experiences: an uneasiness and a solution:

1) The uneasiness, reduced to its simplest terms, is a sense that there is *something wrong about* us as we naturally stand.

2) The solution is a sense that *we are saved from this wrongness* by making proper connection with the higher power.[75]

The essence of religious experience consists in curing the feeling of loss by saving contact with a higher being. This contact occurs when the person dies to his old self and is born again to his real self. James proposes that perhaps this real self is able to contact the higher power because the real self is "coterminous and continuous with *more* of the same quality, which is operative in the universe,"[76] e.g., the higher power. The question of the objective truth[77] of the common noetic core of religious belief centers on the "more of the same quality" which the higher, real self contacts. What definite facts does "the more" instantiate—does the divine exist, what is it, and does it act? James hypothesizes that, "the 'more' with which, in religious experience we feel ourselves connected, is on its *hither* side the subconscious continuation of our conscious life."[78] James contends in religious experience, our subconscious self becomes one with what it was always—the higher power. In other words, James proposes that in religious experience our real self communicates (and in mystical states becomes one with) the divine who is a continuation of our subconscious. Psychological investigation has shown the existence and reality of a wider, subconscious self—"the fact that our conscious power is continuous with a (i.e., the subject's own) wider self through which saving experience comes, . . . it seems to me, is literally and objectively true as far as it goes."[79] There seems to be a sufficient warrant for the reality of our higher self, conceived as our subconscious. But does the "more," which our subconscious contacts, exist; does God exist and is he the extension of our subconscious? James submits that for the mystic there seems to be a sufficient warrant for this belief; but, for those not favored with a "vision" of God and the unseen world, belief in God must be termed an overbelief, a belief without sufficient evidence. However, for the nonmystic there is still some warrant for belief in God—he has the right to believe in God. James here returns to his position that if a belief satisfies our needs and is aligned with our other beliefs, we are justified in believing in it if this belief produces in us real effects. Hence God and the unseen world are real insofar as they produce in us real effects:

> That which produces effects within another reality must be termed a reality itself, so I feel as if we had no philosophic excuse for calling the unseen or mystical world unreal . . . God is real for he produces real effects.[80]

These real effects are several. We have considered the dramatic effects of sainthood—belief in a just and loving God who guarantees an ideal moral order, produces an increase in moral energy and the assurance that we are saved and the world is aright, and so produces a distinct feeling of joy and peace in the believer.

It seems at this point James has gained no ground, for he has reduced the truth of the noetic content of religious belief to subjective utility. Recall that James' evaluation of religious feeling amounted to a judgment that since religious sentiment responded to human needs and produced real effects in the conduct of men's lives it was valuable. He then turned to an evaluation of the truth of the *noetic* content of religious belief to establish what concrete facts these beliefs instantiated. He concluded that belief in the reality of God was an overbelief (warranted only for the mystic) except that this belief produced in the believer real effects. Hence it appears that James has reduced both religious *feeling* and the *noetic content* of belief to subjective *utility* or personal value. That is, he has appraised religious deliverances (both feeling and thought) only in terms of the needs and desires which generated these beliefs. To phrase the objection in another way, if belief in God amounts to only subjective utility, this belief is only an ad hoc hypothesis for it does not cover any *new facts*; instead, it only accounts for a single set of facts—the religious needs and desires of the believer which generated these beliefs.

James faces this objection by arguing that belief in God does postulate new facts. One of these facts has already been indicated—belief in God and prayerful communion with him, raises the believer's moral energy, encouraging him to produce new moral facts. James holds that the charge that this type of fact is only "subjective" must not be allowed:

> As soon as we deal with private and personal phenomena as such, we deal with realities in the completest sense of the term . . . a concrete bit of personal experience may be a small bit, but it is a solid bit as long as it lasts; not hollow, not a mere abstract element of experience, such as the "object" is when taken all alone. It is a *full* fact, even though it be an insignificant fact, it is the kind to which all realities whatsoever must belong.[81]

Persons and their states of consciousness are as valuable and objective as other so-called "objective" facts. Another fact which belief in God postulates is personal immortality. The believer's impulse to increase the amount of good in the world is strengthened by his belief that God is not only presently friendly to our purposes and concerns but that his care and concern will be continued eternally. Moreover even though God may not be omnipotent and infinite, he is our superior with whom we cooperate in creating a novel, ongoing world.

James' answers to the objection that God as an ad hoc hypothesis (explaining only subjective religious sentiments) are particularly elliptic and unsettling. The reason for this deficiency is that these answers are only outlines of theories James develops in his mature metaphysical and epistemological writings. For example, his position that states of consciousness are as equally real, "objective" facts as ordinary things located in space and time, is the germinal statement of his notion of "pure experience"—the central concept of his *Essays in Radical Empiricism*.

Likewise, the notions of the finite God, meliorism and the ongoing universe are pivotal concepts in his *A Pluralistic Universe*. James' attempts to reduce notions and beliefs to their practical consequences issues in his pragmatic theories of meaning and truth in *Pragmatism*. Finally, his evaluation of religious experiences, in the end, returns to his position on the nature of belief. He has argued that the only criteria we have to assess our beliefs are the demands of our passional nature and the corrective pressure of experience. However, in religious belief, the experience consequent upon a belief does not so much correct our beliefs as serve to verify them; in other words, "experience" is corrective only within the level of reality believed in. He contends that desires and interests actually determine what we shall experience. This position on the nature and effect of man's passional nature controlling our experience of reality is an articulation of James' final humanistic philosophy expressed in *The Meaning of Truth*. With these indications of his mature philosophical positions in mind, we turn to our next chapter— "man" in James' metaphysics and epistemology.

4

James' humanistic epistemology and metaphysics

I n this chapter we shall examine James' mature philosophy. Our interest is not in his epistemology and metaphysics per se, but in his later philosophy as a *development* of his theory of man. There will be two sections: James' pragmatic humanism, and James' radical empiricism.

In the section on pragmatism, we will show that even though James credits C. S. Peirce with the original discovery of the principle of pragmatism (as a theory of meaning), James' own distinctive interpretation of this principle has its philosophical foundation in his own theory of man. Secondly, we will examine James' pragmatic theory of truth as an articulation of his final philosophy of humanism.

In the section on James' doctrine of radical empiricism, we will argue that he formulates a metaphysics which is both a development of and a support for his theory of man. As an epistemology, he suggests that radical empiricism's doctrine of "pure experience" can account for the instrumental character of human knowing. He argues that because ideas function by leading us from one experience through and to other experiences, knowledge can be explained in terms of an experienced,

115

conjunctive relation *within* experience. Secondly, since our ideas guide our active interaction with reality, he argues that radical empiricism's metaphysical claim that the world is open, unfinished and susceptible to novel additions is both true to our perceptual experience and consonant with the experiences of the "whole man."

JAMES' PRAGMATIC HUMANISM

In 1898 James delivered a lecture at the University of California entitled "Philosophical Conceptions and Practical Results." In this lecture he expressed the philosophical methodology he had long used. He held that since thought's purpose was to mediate between incoming impressions and outgoing responses, thought's function was to provide an appropriate guide for action. In this lecture, delivered to the Philosophical Union at Berkeley, James quotes C. S. Peirce's statement of 1878 that "the sole meaning of thought is . . . the production of belief. . . . Beliefs, in short, are really rules for action; and the whole function of thought is but one step in the production of habits of action."[1] Peirce suggested that one could determine the meaning of a concept by discovering "what conduct it is fitted to produce."[2] In short, Peirce argued that we can make our ideas clear by determining the conceivable practical effects, i.e., what conduct the ideas prepare us for. James endorses this principle for determining the meanings of concept with the following qualification. He suggests that a concept dicates specific conduct because "it first foretells some particular turn in our experience which shall call for that conduct from us."[3] James proposes that we can discover a concept's meaning by determining what particular experiences it will issue in:

> the effective meaning of any philosophical proposition can always be brought down to some *particular* consequence in our future practical experience, whether active or passive;

the point lying rather in that fact that the experience must
be particular, than in the fact that it must be active.[4]

Pragmatism is then, first of all, a methodological principle for
determining the meanings of concepts.

 James' Berkeley lecture, much like Peirce's original declara-
tions of pragmatism,[5] generated little interest. Six years later
James slightly revised the lecture and it was published in the
Journal of Philosophy.[6] In the same year, James had argued in
an essay "Humanism and Truth,"[7] that if the pragmatic method
is used to determine the meaning of "truth" it will be found to
consist in very definite and specifiable practical satisfactions.
"Pragmatism" was then applied to both a theory of truth and a
theory of meaning. In 1906–7 James delivered the Lowell
Lectures at Boston; these lectures were published as *Pragmatism*.

 Pragmatism sparked a lively controversy.[8] Negative cri-
tiques were published by B. Russell, G. E. Moore and F. H.
Bradley; and to James' defense came Peirce, Dewey, and Schiller.
Although Peirce, James, Dewey, and Schiller did not espouse a
single theory of pragmatism, the pragmatist/antipragmatist controversy encouraged them to present a single, "orthodox"
position.[9] Our aim in the following treatment of pragmatism is
to analyze the distinctive position of James. We will argue that as
a *theory of meaning*, James' pragmatism was a natural development of his previous thought. In short, James' pragmatic theory
of meaning not only was employed in his psychological, ethical,
and religious thought but also the *philosophical basis* for it was
his philosophy of man. James' pragmatic *theory of truth*, we will
suggest, is a generalization of his theory of man and is an
articulation of his mature philosophy of "humanism."

James' pragmatic theory of meaning

 He begins his Lowell Lectures by explaining that pragmatism is a methodological principle for clarifying the meaning of

words.[10] He suggests that interminable philosophical disputes can be settled by discovering the practical consequences of the notions involved:

> What difference would it practically make to anyone if this notion rather than that notion were true? If no practical difference whatever can be traced, then the alternatives mean practically the same thing and all dispute is idle.[11]

James not only recommends this pragmatic method for solving metaphysical disputes, he suggests that if no practical consequences accrue from an idea, that concept is meaningless: "if it can make no practical difference whether a given statement be true or false, then the statement has not real meaning."[12] At this point, pragmatism, as a method for determining the meanings of words and settling metaphysical disputes, looks like little more than traditional empiricism. James acknowledges this by naming as predecessors Aristotle, Locke, Berkeley, and Hume and by subtitling his volume "A New Name for Some Old Ways of Thinking."

James suggests that pragmatism involves a new orientation in that it conceives philosophy to be a practical, concrete problem-solving enterprise:

> The whole function of philosophy ought to be to find out what difference it would make to you and to me at definite instances in our life, if this world-formula or that world-formula would be true.[13]

Further, this view of philosophy as a practical pursuit is based on an instrumental view of human knowledge. As we have seen in his psychology, James argued that thought's function consists in mediating between impressions and reactions. James argued that ideas as summaries of past experience guide future action.

Hence his proposal that the meaning of ideas consists in *concrete consequences* constitutes an application of the view of man developed in his psychology.[14]

This instrumental view of knowledge holds that the meaning of an idea is not established by reducing it to the sense impressions from which it was derived; rather, meanings are to be located in the *consequences* of an idea or belief. We have already indicated that James amended Peirce's position (that ideas mean general rules for conduct) to his own stand that meanings can be reduced to a particular consequence in our future experience. James' pragmatism is hence distinctive in its holding that "conceivable effects" refer to sensations and particular concrete experiences. James argues that the meaning of a concept is determined by considering:

> What conceivable effects of a practical kind the object may involve—what sensations we are to expect from it and what reactions we must prepare. Our conception of these effects, whether immediate or remote, is then for us the whole of our conception of the object.[15]

Although this reference to particular sense experiences exemplifies James' stress on individuality (as opposed to Peirce's stress on generality and a community of inquirers), there is another distinctive Jamesian strain that has generally been overlooked.

James begins his Lowell Lectures with a discussion of the two prevailing tendencies in philosophy. He characterizes them as follows: "tender-minded" (rationalist, i.e., going by principles, intellectualistic, idealistic, monistic, religious, free willistic, dogmatical) and "tough-minded" (empiricist, i.e., going by facts, sensationalistic, materialistic, pluralistic, irreligious, fatalistic, skeptical). He then proposes that pragmatism is a *media via* between these two tendencies. Although James' initial articulation of pragmatism considered the meaning of religious language, his pragmatism was characterized as a "tough-minded" orientation. Despite his reference to the "cash value" meanings of concepts, James gives particular stress to a pragmatic reduction of concepts to aesthetic, ethical, and religious experiences. In the following we shall briefly examine several examples which show James' distinctive emphasis on the concrete experiences of the "whole man."

In his Berkeley lecture, James examines the metaphysical option—materialism or theism. He first poses the hypothetical case of deciding this option in the last moment of time in the universe. In this instance since there is no possibility of future conceivable effects, there is no pragmatic difference between believing the world to be matter or a creation of God: "Thus if no *future* detail of experience or conduct is to be deduced from our hypothesis, the debate between materialism and theism becomes quite idle and insignificant."[16] However if we take the world as it is, with a future before it, the theism/materialism option becomes meaningful. The difference believing in God makes is a difference in expectation. The believer's hopes are defined, for a permanent moral order is guaranteed:

> Here then, in these different emotional and practical appeals, in these adjustments of our concrete attitudes of hope and expectation, and all the delicate consequences which their differences entail, lies the real meaning of materialism and theism. . . . Materialism means simply the denial that the moral order is eternal moral order and the letting loose of hope.[17]

The consequences of belief in God consist in definite experiences in the believer. James also notes, as we have seen above, that the delineation of God's moral attributes (as opposed to his metaphysical ones) is meaningful because it involves definite experience and defines the conduct of the believer. Hence, for James, "conceivable effects" include religious experiences.

In his psychology and ethics James has given several other instances of notions being pragmatically traced to concrete experiences of the "whole man." For example, the option between the interactionist and the conscious automaton theories was reduced to a concrete consequence—the ability of the interactionists to account by their views for our concrete experience of consciousness's efficacy in positing ends and directing behavior. In the matter of ethics, the pragmatic difference between determinism and indeterminism was reduced to indeterminism's ability to support moral experience, our concrete experiences of impugnability and novelty.

James proposes his pragmatic theory of meaning as a method of determining the meanings of concepts (hence, resolving metaphysical disputes) by tracing the differing conceivable effects which would occur if the concept were true. This experiential, fact-orientated approach differs from traditional empiricism in that it embodies an instrumental view of mind which holds that the function of thought is to guide future actions. James' pragmatism is distinctive in that he understands "conceivable effects" to apply to concrete experiences. Further, he is careful not to restrict these concrete experiences to practical, sensible effects, instead he argues that aesthetic, moral, and religious experiences can pragmatically define a concept.

Pragmatism as a theory of truth

James begins his theory of truth in a decidedly noncontroversial way. He states that truth is a property of certain of our ideas—true ideas agree with reality, false ones do not. So far the pragmatist and the antipragmatist agree; the pragmatist, however, requires that "agreement" be concretely defined.

One way of agreeing with reality is achieved when our ideas "copy" reality—such is the case in sense knowledge, suggests James. However most of our true ideas do not "copy" reality. How then do we decide the truth or falsity of those noncopying ideas? James proposes that true ideas "lead satis-factorily":

> Agreement turns out to be essentially an affair of leading—leading that is useful because it is into quarters that contain objects that are important. True ideas lead us into useful verbal and conceptual quarters as well as directly up to useful sensible termini.[18]

In short, James suggests that "truth" is an abstract noun which refers to ideas which successfully guide our behavior. Further, James argues that truth is not a static relation between our ideas and reality, rather, truths are "made":

> The truth of an idea is not a stagnant property inherent in it. Truth *happens* to an idea. It *becomes* true, is *made* true by events. Its verity *is*, in fact, an event, a process: the process, namely, of its verifying itself, its veri*fication*. Its validity is the process of vali*dation*.[19]

Truth is created by the interaction between the knower and reality.

James' theory met almost instant and complete rejection. This reception was partly due to the theory's novelty and partly due to its nontechnical exposition (*Pragmatism* consisted of published lectures). For two years James and his critics stated and restated their cases. In 1909 James collected his articles on truth in a volume entitled *The Meaning of Truth*. Our interest, however, is not in the pragmatist/antipragmatist controversy. Since our concern is with James' distinctive theory of truth, we will restrict our discussion to two considerations: his theory of truth as a development of his philosophy of man, and his theory of truth as "humanism."

1. *James' theory of truth as a development of his philosophy of man.* In our previous section we have seen how James' position on the instrumentality of the mind was fundamental to his theory of meaning. He proposed that ideas as summaries and reconstructions of past experience function as guides to future experience. His theory of truth suggests that the truth or falsity of an idea is determined by its successfully leading to new experiences. "Success," however, must also be pragmatically defined for it, too, is an abstract notion which is applied to many sorts of beneficial experiences. In general, then, James' theory of truth consists in an analysis of the variety of ways our ideas "successfully lead."

How do we judge success? James contends that success cannot be judged without reference to some purpose or interest. Hence the structure of interests and purposes of the knower provides the criterion for judgments of success. Since human purposes range from the practical, survival-oriented to the higher ethical and religious interests, the judgment of an idea's "successfully leading" must be made in relation to the interest in question.

Most obvious of the human interests is survival. James has suggested that "ascertainment of outward fact" is crucial for this purpose:

> The importance to human life of having true beliefs about matters of fact is a thing *too notorious*. We live in world of realities that can be infinitely useful or infinitely harmful. Ideas that tell us which of them to expect count as true ideas in all this primary sphere of verification, and the pursuit of such ideas is a primary human duty.[20]

The mere ascertainment of outward fact constitutes only one form of satisfying vital needs. James proposes that a far more important mode of our ideas "agreeing" with reality is their guiding function:

> [ideas guide us] straight up to or into its [reality's] surround-ings; or put [us] into such working touch with it as to handle either it or something connected with it better than if we disagreed.[21]

Here again we see the central strain in James' pragmatism. Our true ideas, prompted by survival interests, lead us to experiences which successfully lead to the satisfaction of those interests.

> Any idea that will carry us prosperously forth from any one part of our experience to any other part, linking things satisfactorily, working securely, simplifying, saving labor, is true for just so much, true in so far forth, true *instrumentally*.[22]

On this basic, common sense level, then, in response to our most practical needs, our ideas are true if they lead success-fully to other parts of experience. On this most basic level, the corrective pressure of reality (experienced via sense knowledge) is the most obvious criterion of truth and falsity. James' distinctive pragmatic theory of truth comes to the fore when he turns to the satisfaction of our other interests—aesthetical, ethical, and religious.

At the beginning of our section on James' religious thought we examined his theory of the nature and legitimacy of belief. His pragmatic theory of truth, with reference to the interests of the "whole man," is an elaboration of this theory of belief. Our judgment of satisfaction of these "higher" interests involves several criteria. We saw, for example, that even though *scientific theories* must "fit" reality, the interests of our passional nature play an important part. The satisfactoriness of two rival theories is often judged on purely subjective grounds—e.g., simplicity, elegance, etc. Another subjective consideration which bears on our judgment of a new theory is its "fit" with our old stock of theories. James describes the process by which old theories are overturned and new ones put in their place: a novel experience puts a strain on our old theories, i.e., the new fact is incompatible with or contradicts the old theory. At this point, the inquirer may dismiss the new fact or he may adjust his old theory:

> He saves as much of it [his previous theory] as he can, for in this matter of belief, we are all extreme conservatives. So he tries to first change this opinion, then that, until some new idea comes up which he can graft upon the ancient stock with a minimum of disturbance to the latter, some idea that mediates between the stock and the new experience and runs them into one another most felicitously and expediently.[23]

James argues that the importance given to new facts, or conversely the importance given to old theories, along with the judgment of the satisfactoriness of the new theory are all subjective considerations which are evaluated in terms of the interests and desires of the knower,

> A new opinion counts as "true" just in proportion as it gratifies the individual's desire to assimilate the novel in his experience to his beliefs in stock. It must both lean on old truth and grasp new fact; and its success in doing this, is a matter for the individual's appreciation. When old truth grows, then, by a new truth's addition, it is for subjective reasons. . . . That new idea is truest which performs most felicitously its function of satisfying our double urgency. It makes itself true, gets itself classed as true, by the way it

works; grafting itself then upon the ancient body of truth.[24]

This subjective judgment of the satisfactoriness of the new theory does not give the inquirer license to believe according to his wishes. The inquirer is coerced both by the corrective pressure of future experiences and by his old stock of truths:

> Pent in, as the pragmatist is . . . between the whole body of funded truths squeezed from the past and coercions of the world of sense about him, who so well as he feels the immense pressure of objective control under which our minds perform their operations.[25]

James suggests that the criteria of satisfactoriness governing the attribution "true" to opinions and beliefs (here, in particular, scientific theories) can be specified in terms of definite criteria (successfully leading to new experiences and consistency with old theories) which are judged to be satisfied by a subjective judgment of the inquirer. He concludes that not only are rival theories judged on subjective grounds (simplicity, elegance) but that the respective importance given to either the old theory or to the new fact is a subjective judgment. He next turns to ethical and religious truths.

James' position is that the function of thought is the fixation of belief and since the fixation of belief leads to action, in some cases belief may actually create its own verification. Above we saw that James argued that belief in a melioristic universe and God may actually create its own verification. Here he gives us a more common example—trust in another person helps create trustworthiness:

> Our judgments, at any rate, change the character of *future* reality by the acts to which they lead. Where these acts are

experiences of trust—trust, e.g., that a man is honest, that
our health is good enough, or that we can make a successful effort,—which acts may be a needed antecedent of the
trusted thing's becoming true.[26]

In these cases of "will to believe" the satisfactoriness of a belief
is judged by the same criteria: the demands of future experience, old beliefs, and the needs and interests of the inquirer.
However, old beliefs and the needs and interests of the inquirer in these cases of "will to believe" do not so much
measure the satisfactoriness of the new belief as they actually do
help to create the verification of the new belief. Recall James'
example that belief in God promotes an increase in moral energy,
thereby increasing in us our sense of the presence and purposes
of God.

James' theory of truth proposes that the ideas agree with
reality. He argues that "agreement" can be made meaningful
only through an examination of the various ways ideas satis-
factorily lead to concrete experiences. "Satisfactoriness" in turn,
must be analyzed with reference to specific interests and purposes. On the basic common sense level, the satisfactoriness of
ideas is chiefly judged in terms of the success of our future
experiences. We cannot believe what we choose, for reality
coerces beliefs by its corrective pressure. However, as we proceed to the experiences of the "whole man" the corrective pressure of reality is supplemented by other criteria—the demand for
consistency with our old truths and the demands of our interests.
In the special case of ethical and religious beliefs, the demands
of our passional nature encourage actions which help to create
the realities which can verify our initial beliefs.

A whole battery of criticisms was leveled at James' theory.
We shall consider only two. Many antipragmatists charged that
the pragmatist's stress on the role of interests and desires in
determining the satisfactoriness of future experiences, allowed

the pragmatist to count as true any belief or theory which satisfied any desire. James responded that the attribution "true" to certain of our ideas was no more arbitrary for the pragmatist than for the antipragmatist. For example, in our choice of theories,

> [these man-made formulas], we cannot be capricious with impunity any more than can we be capricious on the common-sense practical level. We must find a theory that will *work*; and that means something extremely difficult; for our theory must mediate between all previous truths and certain new experiences. It must derange common sense and previous belief as little as possible, and it must lead to some sensible terminus or other that can be verified exactly. To "work" means both these things; and the squeeze is so tight that there is little loose play for any hypothesis.[27]

James answers, in short, that all the pragmatist has done is to make specific the criteria by which anyone judges theories to be satisfactory. Further, he suggests that the pragmatist has been honest enough to acknowledge the role of subjective, human interests in our choice of theories.

A second common charge was that the "success," "workableness," "satisfactoriness," etc., were only *signs* of the truth which pre-exists. James answers by making three points. First, he suggests that the pragmatists have given a concrete account of what the antipragmatist refers to, in the abstract, as truth; also he challenges his objectors to indicate concretely what remains of the truth-relation once its satisfactoriness has been pragmatically traced to concrete experiences. Secondly, James argues that truths do not simply copy reality but that they are human additions to reality. Finally, James argues that even if Truth be a prehuman, *ante rem* standard which we ought to follow, "the only guarantee that we shall in fact follow (that standard) must lie in our human equipment . . . the existence of any amount of reality *ante rem* is no warrant against unlimited error *in rebus* being incurred."[28] In short, James argues that the human contribution intrudes into all our thinking to such an extent that a theory of truth is really a theory of man—a humanism.

2. *James' theory of truth as a "humanism."* The term "humanism" was first applied to the pragmatic theory of truth by Schiller; James found the term apt: "I think Mr. Schiller's proposal to call the wider pragmatism [i.e., the theory of truth] by the name of 'humanism' is excellent and ought to be adopted."[29] Although James frequently refers to his "humanistic" theory of truth, he adds that, unfortunately, "pragmatism" became the accepted term.

Basically "humanism" holds that the human element pervades all our thinking: "it is impossible to strip the *human element* out from even our most abstract theorizing."[30] James argues that all our truths are man-made products:

> to an unascertainable extent our truths are man-made products. Human motives sharpen all our questions, human satisfaction lurk in all our answers, all our formulas have a human twist.[31]

James' systematic exposition ("Pragmatism and Humanism")[32] of the impact of the human element in our thinking is another attempt to express his position on the nature of truth's "agreement" with reality.

He suggests that truths must take account of three parts of reality: the flux of sensations; the relations that obtain between our sensations and their "copies" in our mind (these relations being of two types: the first, mutable relations like time and place and the second, fixed relations which obtain because of the meanings attached to words); and finally our previous stock of truths. James argues that these three parts of reality correct our beliefs only within the human perspective.

In his psychology, he has argued that consciousness's selectivity according to human interests extends to even our sensation and perception of sensible reality. Recall his example that when we look at a table top, even though the retinal sensation is of two acute and obtuse angles, we actually *see* a square table. He holds that, "even in the field of sensation, our minds exert a certain arbitrary choice."[33] Even at this most basic level, human interests "filter" our experience of reality's corrective pressure.

The relations between our ideas and matters of fact are obviously mutable and dependent upon our temporary purposes. Recall, that in his analysis of conception and reasoning, James argued that all our conceptions are temporary and are adequate solely for a specific purpose, e.g., paper is essentially a combustible material or a writing surface, depending on one's purpose. He concluded that our conceptions *"characterize us more than they characterize things."*[34] Although the relations based on the meanings of words are not temporary and mutable, they obviously betray the limitations of specific purposes:

> There are so many geometries, so many logics . . . so many classifications, each one of them good for so much and yet not good for everything, that the notion that even the truest formula may be a human device and not a literal transcript has dawned on us.[35]

James concludes that the second part of reality (relations between sensations and their "copies" in our mind) which our truths must take account of, also bear the imprint of human interests and purposes.

The third part of reality our truths must take account of is our old stock of truths. The new facts we encounter are already *funded* with our previous truths:

> It is therefore, only the smallest and recentest fraction of the first two parts of reality that comes to us without the human touch, and *that fraction has immediately to become humanized* in the sense of being squared, assimilated, or in some way adapted, *to the humanized mass already there*.[36]

James proposes that the human factor is so pervasive that we never encounter reality-in-itself. Recall his point that we are not able to notice a feature completely foreign to us, we must be first told what it "looks like" before we can see it. Humanism holds that truths are human products made within the tissue of human experience. Since the function of ideas is to lead us from the more familiar, more fixed parts of experience to the novel, less fixed parts of experience, ideas which successfully lead are deemed true. James' theory of truth holds that "successful leading" can only be defined in the concrete and that success is measured in terms of satisfying the human interests which originally prompted inquiry.

To those critics who charge that this theory of truth is too subjective, James counters by indicating the pervasiveness of the human contribution. He argues that at every level where reality, needs, or past truths exert corrective pressure on our beliefs, the human element "filters" this corrective pressure. Even on the most basic, common-sense level, the human element shapes our experience of reality. In short, James proposes that all our experience is theory-laden—the theory in question being the structure of interests and purposes in man's nature. All our truths betray the human coefficient: "all our truths, even the most elemental, are affected by race-inheritance with a human coefficient."[37] All our truths are human products.

Truths are created by the dialectic of man's passional nature legislating beliefs and reality responding with corrective pressure. The pragmatist argues that truths are *provisional* hypotheses, whose success can only be evaluated with reference to specific purposes. Even though a new theory be considered more adquate, the old theory may still remain true—given the context and purposes in reference to which it was framed. For example, since an idea's truth depends on the satisfactoriness of its practical consequences, it is still true that the world is flat, i.e., when sailing from France to England, the shortest route is a straight line, not the great circle route. This paradoxical state of affairs did not bother James, for he held that there is not one immutable Truth, rather, there are many truths and the satisfactoriness of each of them can only be evaluated in terms of concrete practical consequences, in view of definite purposes.

James suggests that his view of truth holds that reality tolerates the human addition, "We add, both to the subject and to the predicate part of reality. The world stands really malleable, waiting to receive its final touches at our hands."[38] In short, James' view of truth involves a definite view of the world —his theory of truth awaits the metaphysical underpinnings of *A Pluralistic Universe*. Also, James' view of truth proposes that ideas and reality are equally parts of experience; true ideas successfully guide us within experience. He argues that no reference outside human experience is needed:

> Tho one part of experience may lean upon another part to make it what it is in any one of several respects in which it may be considered, experience as a whole is self-containing and leans on nothing. . . . Humanism is willing to let finite experience be self-supporting.[39]

Hence, James' theory of truth also awaits the epistemology of "pure experience" expressed in *Essays in Radical Empiricism*.

JAMES' RADICAL EMPIRICISM

In the preface of *The Meaning of Truth*, James writes that although most of the pragmatist/antipragmatist controversy has been "verbal wrangling"[40] he feels it advantageous to collect his responses to the critics into a volume. He states that his interest is not in the pragmatic theory of truth, per se but in a metaphysical doctrine—radical empiricism:

> it seems to me that the establishment of the pragmatic theory of truth is a step of first rate importance in making radical empiricism prevail.[41]

James summarizes this metaphysical position[42] by saying that radical empiricism consists in three theses: a postulate, a statement of fact, and a generalized conclusion.

First of all, radical empiricism *postulates* that the subject matter of philosophy shall be all things experienced or experienceable:

> Nothing shall be admitted as fact except what can be experienced at some definite time by some experient; and for every feature of fact ever so experienced, a definite place must be found somewhere in the final system of reality. In other words, everything real must be experienceable somewhere, and every kind of thing experienced must somewhere be real.[43]

Radical empiricism aligns itself with the "fact-orientated" empirical philosophies which have held that the touchstone of reality is experience. James joins those philosophers who have held that experience shall be the final judge of the validity of theoretical constructions. The radicality of James' empiricism is expressed in its second thesis.

Radical empiricism holds as *a matter of fact* that conjunctive relations between things are experienced just as certainly as the things they join:

> The conjunctions are as primordial elements of "fact" as are the distinctions and disjunctions. In the same act by which I feel that this passing minute is a new pulse in my life, I feel that the old life is continued into it, and the feeling of continuance in no wise jars upon the simultaneous feeling of a novelty. They, too compenetrate harmoniously. Prepositions, copulas and conjunctions, "is," "isn't," "then," "before," "in," "on," "besides," "between," "next," "like," "unlike," "as," "but," flower out of the stream of pure experience, the stream of concretes or the sensation stream, as naturally as nouns and adjectives do.[44]

James proposes that conjunctive relations need not be imposed from an extra-experiential, a priori source; rather, experience itself contains these relations. Since things experienced are real, these relations are real, i.e., part of reality, the generalized conclusion follows.

Radical empiricism concludes that reality as it is experienced is self-sustaining, "the directly apprehended universe needs, in short, no extraneous, trans-empirical connective support, but possesses in its own right a concatenated or continuous structure."[45] James concludes that reality is, as we experience it, a "loose-jointed unity," with differing degrees of both intimacy and externality.

James submits that if we accept radical empiricism's postulate (that all experienced things are real) and if we analyze our experience of conjunctive relations, we will discover solutions to many of the most difficult problems of metaphysics. Since our interest is in James' metaphysics as it relates to his philosophy of man, the remainder of this chapter will consider two areas: radical empiricism's account of the "experience" and radical empiricism's discussion of the nature of the universe.

Radical empiricism: an epistemology of pure experience

Before we begin our treatment of this rather technical and difficult aspect of James' thought, we should make clear its important function in our general treatment of James. We have argued that James' initial philosophical concern was in framing a theory of man and that his mature epistemology and metaphysics provide explication and justification of this view of man. At several points we have seen James either take provisional stands or postpone critical problems. It is now time to test the "cash value" of these promissory notes. Accordingly we treat at some length his epistemology of "pure experience" and its application to specific problems in his theory of man.

One of the fundamental notions in James' theory of man is his position on the instrumental character of the mind. In *Essays in Radical Empiricism*, James works out an epistemology consonant with this view of mind. In *Pragmatism*, he has argued that knowledge does not so much represent reality as put us into "working touch" with it. Here, he will argue that with a correct analysis of perceptual knowledge, the traditional problem of the "gap" between the knower and the known can be avoided. He proposes that if reality be considered "pure experience," from one context a "bit" of experience is "subject" and from another, "object,"[46] In short, he suggests that the subject/object distinction is a *functional* not an entitative distinction. He then discusses the role of conceptual knowledge in leading us back to acquaintance-knowledge of reality. Our treatment will be divided into three sections: reality as pure experience and perceptual knowledge, conceptual knowledge as ministerial to perceptual knowledge, and experience and the existence of the self.

1. *Reality as pure experience and perceptual knowledge.* James begins by describing the world in the most general terms. Rather than beginning with the categories "thought" and "thing" and then attempting to reduce one to the other, James proposes to describe the world by what he calls a "double-barrelled term"—experience. He then argues that the world, as it is experienced, presents no duality; reality is pure, neutral experience:

> "pure experience" is the name which I give to the immediate flux of life which furnishes the material to our later reflection with its conceptual categories. Only new-born babes, or men in a semi-coma from sleep, drugs, illness or blows, may be assumed to have an experience pure in the literal sense of *that* which is not yet any definite *what*. . . . Its purity is only a relative term, meaning the proportional amount of unverbalized sensation which it still embodies.[47]

James confesses having difficulty describing what this pure, undifferentiated experience is. He says that it is not a general stuff of which experience is made. It is experience itself; it is a collective name for all sensible natures—"it is made of *that*, of just what appears, of space, of intensity, of flatness, of brownness, heaviness, or what not."[48] The importance of James' identification of pure experience and sensible natures that his novel reconstruction of the knowledge-relation resolves one of our postponed problems.

In *The Principles of Psychology*, James suggested that our perceptual "acquaintance-knowledge" (as distinguished from conceptual "knowledge-about") reveals the nature of reality. He now explains that this is so because in perceptual knowledge there is an identification between what exists and what is known. Subjectively a "bit" of pure experience represents; objectively, it is represented:

> What represents and what is represented is here necessarily the same; but we must remember that no dualism of being represented and representing resides in experience *per se*. In its pure state, or when isolated, there is no self-splitting of it into consciousness and what the consciousness is "of." Its subjectivity and objectivity are *functional* attributes solely, realized only when the experience is "taken," i.e., talked of, twice, considered with two differing contexts.[49]

James suggests that in the instant field of the present, our awareness is only of pure experience. Retroactively, and only by way of addition do we separate pure experience into "subject" and "object." James' interest is not in eliminating the subject/object distinction in order to return to undifferentiated experience. Rather, he proposes that if this distinction be considered *functional*, there will be no intrinsic difference of natures to create the gap between subject and object.

James gives several illustrations in which the subject/object distinction can be construed as functional. He notes the "shifting place of secondary qualities in the history of philosophy."[50] He suggests that if "mental" and "physical" meant two different kinds of intrinsic nature, no ambiguity should have occurred. In response to practical needs, proposes James, color, heat, sound, etc., function as properties of the object; it is only in response to more advanced intellectual and theoretical needs that these qualities are deemed properties of the subject. James lists as another example of the functional attribution of "subject" and "object," our experience of our body. My body is sometimes considered an object; at other times, it is not my possession—it is me. In Marcel's words, the body is at the crossroads of subject and object. James concludes that these examples indicate that the ambiguity of the terms "subject" and "object" is natural for these terms indicate not differing natures but differing functions.

How can one "bit" of pure experience function as subject and object or as consciousness and content? James argues that in perceptual knowledge, thought-stuff and thing-stuff are indistinguishable. Since we are here dealing with immediate, acquaintance knowledge, our perception does not represent or point—it puts us into direct contact with the things:

> The paper seen and the seeing of it are only two names for one indivisible fact, which properly named is, *the datum, the phenomenon, or the experience*. The paper is in the mind and the mind is around the paper, because paper and mind are only two names that are given later to one experience, when, taken in a larger world of which it forms a part, its connections are traced in different directions.[51]

The experience, here, the paper, is a bit of pure experience which is a part of two great associative systems—the experiencer's mental biography and the experienced facts of the world. James offers the model below.

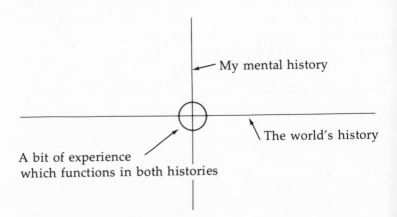

Given the context of the associative system in question, the paper functions either as a part of the world or as a part of the experiencer. The paper both is and is known at the intersection of the two histories. Following his model, James suggests that because many lines may pass through a point in the world's history, the paper is a shared experience, i.e., it may also function in another experiencer's mental history. James proposes that in perceptual acquaintance-knowledge, "mental-content and object [are] identical."[52] Hence, concludes James, by taking only our *experience* of the conjunctive relation we call "knowing," he is able to explain perceptual knowledge in terms of a bit of pure experience operating differently in two contexts. If "subject" and "object" be terms which distinguish different functions rather than intrinsic, entitative differences, new light is shed on a problem which occurred in his religious thought.

In his defense of belief in God, James had argued that belief is warranted if it produces in us real effects, i.e., the unseen world is real at least insofar as it produces real effects. In answer to the charge that belief in God was an ad hoc hypothesis, i.e., it did not encompass any new facts, it only accounted for the needs and desires which generated the initial belief, James proposed that it did indeed cover new facts, namely the believer's feeling of assurance and his increased moral energy. He responded to the charge that those new facts were merely "subjective" by claiming that states of consciousness were as equally real as other, so-called "objective" facts.

In his doctrine of "pure experience," James provides a metaphysical basis for his claim. He argues that a "bit" of experience can function in either of two contexts—personal biography or world history. In his view, the subjective/objective distinction is not based on a difference of intrinsic nature but rather, it is a functional distinction. Hence, the objection that belief in God is warranted only by the "subjective" effects it produces is neutralized, given James' doctrine of pure experience. In his view, both subjective and objective facts are equally real for they are, in fact, one "bit" of experience given differing contexts.

2. *Conceptual knowledge as ministerial to perceptual knowledge.* The relation of perceptual and conceptual knowledge is an abiding theme in James' thought. In his psychology he argues that acquaintance-knowledge (e.g., an experience of color) is both primary and prior to knowledge-about (e.g., color theory). In his *Pragmatism* he argued that particular acquaintance-experiences define the meaning of an idea and that the truth of an idea is judged according as it successfully leads to a future, concrete acquaintance-experience. In his radical empiricism he again affirms that perceptual knowledge is primary to conceptual knowledge because perceptual knowledge is necessary for survival (whereas conceptual knowledge is not) and since the meanings of concepts must be determined by a perceptual experience. James' radical empiricism, however, does not simply reaffirm his previous stand. He has argued that since the conjunctive relation we term "knowing" is given in experience, ideas function as guides within experience. Our interest is in his explication of how ideas lead *within* experiences.

James suggests that when a concept of X is had in mind, no mysterious "presence in absence" is involved. The concept has a leading function which it exercises by guiding us through a series of intermediaries provided by the context in question. This context may be mental or physical. James gives an example of the pointing function of our idea of tigers in India:

> The pointing of our thought to tigers is known simply and solely as the procession of mental associates and motor consequences that follow on the thought and that would lead harmoniously, if followed out into some ideal or real context, or even into the immediate presence of the tiger.[53]

If the context be mental, we will be able to indicate the differences between tigers and lions. If the context be the physical world, we would bring back tigers (not lions) if we hunted in India. James concludes that the essentials of the cognitive relations, when the knowledge be conceptual, consist in: "intermediary experiences (possible, if not actual) of continuously developing progress, and finally, of fulfillment, when the sensible percept, which is the object, is reached."[54] James illustrates his claim that intermediary experiences constitute the conceptual knowledge-relation by comparing his account with the traditional one.

Since the traditional theories have distinguished subject and object entitively, there is a "gap" between knower and known. Knowledge consists in bridging this gap; this account James terms "saltatory." His account has subject and object being identified in perceptual knowledge (and conceptual knowing leading to perceptual acquaintance), hence, the knowledge-relation can be accounted for *within* experience. Since there is no gap, knowledge consists in moving through intermediary experiences; this account, he terms "ambulatory":

> Cognition, whenever we take it concretely, means determinate "ambulation," through intermediaries, from a *terminus a quo* to a *terminus ad quem* . . . our idea brings us into the object's neighborhood, practical or ideal, gets us into commerce with it, helps us towards its closer acquaintance, enables us to foresee it, class it, compare it, deduce it, in short, to deal with it.[55]

James argues that concepts do not *represent*, they *lead*. The concrete experiences they lead us through are intermediary experiences between one perceptual experience and another.

There are obviously cases in which the return to a perceptual experience is not intended. In these cases, our concepts serve as substitutes for the intermediary experiences. We need not constantly experience the welter of concrete particulars; our concepts, as summaries and reconstructions of past experience, can be experimented with by themselves—return to perceptual experience may be postponed indefinitely. We may deal exclusively in mental context, in order to save ourselves time and trouble, "by letting an idea call up its associates systematically, we may be led to a terminus which the corresponding real term would have led in the case we have operated on the real world."[56] Concepts, then, lead us through the intermediaries provided by the context, be it mental or physical.

In James' view, concepts function by leading us through intermediaries. Yet, whether these intermediaries be mental or physical, the meaning of a concept is determined by reducing it to *future* consequences. An idea predicts certain consequences and then leads us on a procedure of discovery to see if the prediction is true. The predictive accuracy of an idea is based on a generalization of past experience and it is appraised by its success in leading to an acquaintance-experience of concrete particulars.

James, then, takes as primary, perceptual knowledge and as secondary, conceptual knowledge. In *perceptual knowing*, the thing known and the knowing of it is explained in terms of a bit of pure experience which functions differently in two contexts which intersect in the knowing of the thing. *Conceptual knowing* functions by leading us from one immediate, acquaintance-experience to another. Concepts are true when they successfully lead us through the context provided by either our mental system or the given world.

In the minds of many of his contemporaries, James' radical empiricism was, at best, subjectivistic; at worst, solipsistic. The basic charge was that since James conceived knowledge as an experienced relation within experience, no objective reference to the external world was possible. In short, James has us continually experiencing our own subjective experiences, never do we contact external facts.

His response consists in a reaffirmation of his general view of man; in particular, his humanistic pragmatism. He has argued that the human knower is not a disinterested spectator but an involved actor. As an "interested selector" man's knowledge is not a neutral apprehension of a static, finished reality, rather our ideas function as guides for interacting with reality. Our experience of the knowing-relation is of it as a future-orientated process. Since knowing is a process within experience, an extra-experiential reference is unnecessary; past experience suggests hypotheses and future experience confirms, rejects or modifies these hypotheses. In short, James suggests that when seen as a development of his pragmatism, radical empiricism's reference to the *satisfactoriness* of intermediary or terminal experiences insures the transcendency of objects: "the existence of the object, whenever the idea asserts it 'truly,' is the only reason . . . why the idea does work successfully."[57] Radical empiricism, he concludes, is in part, a pragmatic description of the ambulatory character of knowledge, through and to future experiences.

3. *Experience and the existence of the self.* James' whole thought can be characterized as an attempt to satisfy opposite demands, he calls them "tough and tender minded" tendencies. For example, in his psychology he sought an empirical, objective study yet he allowed the demands of the "whole man" to dictate certain stances. We observed his provisional acceptance of passing thought as the thinker since a self was required for man's moral and religious experiences. His pragmatism also reflects this tension. Though he talks of survival orientation, environmental adjustment, and cash-value practicality, his chief concern is with a "pragmatic" analysis of man's nonpractical, higher experiences. His radical empiricism

provides but another example. Its initial premise holds that "nothing shall be admitted as fact except what can be experienced at some definite time by some experient."[58] The final resolution of the question of the existence of the self reflects this tension in James' thought at its extreme. The self required by higher experiences seems not to be experienced; in fact, James begins *Essays in Radical Empiricism* with even a more disturbing doubt, "Does 'Consciousness' exist?"

James suggests that faithfulness to facts indicates that consciousness is *experienced as* a variety of intracephalic and bodily movements of the organism adjusting to its environment. "Consciousness" is apparently only an abstract name for a function, and that function is experienced as physical movements: "the stream of thinking (consciousness) is only a careless name for what when carefully scrutinized, reveals itself to consist chiefly of the stream of my breathing."[59] How then could James accept the existence of the self, which, though demanded by experiences of the "whole man" seems itself not to be experienced?

James was intensely aware of this ambiguity in his thought and since he felt both the tender- and tough-minded demands to be valid, he sought a solution which would allow him to save both demands. This ambiguity, which spanned the whole of his thought,[60] was finally resolved in the last chapter of *A Pluralistic Universe*. In his psychology, he had argued that although our awareness is focused on a *center* of consciousness, that center is continuous with a *fringe* which we are "subconsciously" aware of. He suggests that the same might be the case with the self—although we are only aware of the self *centered* in bodily motions, the self exists continuously as a *fringe* which surrounds this basic, bodily awareness:

What we conceptually identify ourselves with and say we are thinking of at any time is the center (cephalic movements of adjustment); but our *full self* is the whole field, with all those indefinitely radiating subconscious possibilities of increase that we can only feel without conceiving, and hardly begin to analyze.[61]

James suggests that our awareness of the self seems to consist only in our experience of cephalic movements of adjustment since those movements are in response to our most immediate, practical needs:

> The conscious self of the moment, the central self, is probably determined to this privileged position by its functional connection with the body's imminent or present acts. It is the present acting self. Tho the more that surrounds it may be "subconscious" to us, yet if in its "collective capacity" it also exerts an active function, it may be conscious in a wider way.[62]

At this point it seems that the metaphor breaks down for if the wider self is not experienced (i.e., it is simply subconsciously felt), it is not admissible as matter for philosophy according to the postulate of radical empiricism. James suggests that the wider self need not always be only on the fringe, it may move to the center—"the centre works in one way while the margins work in another, and presently [they] overpower the centre and are central themselves."[63] He contends that in the ethical and religious experiences of the "whole man" the wider, spiritual self moves from subconscious to conscious awareness. The self is *experienced as* the source of our experiences of activity and effort. In a word, the self is experienced in the exercise of our free will. Interestingly enough the solution to James' ambiguity was best articulated in an early essay "The Feeling of Effort" (1880). There he argued that the feeling of spontaneous psychic effort which we experience in the exercise of our free-

dom is "this greeting of the spirit, this acquiescence, conniv-
ance, partiality, call it what you will, which seems the inward
gift of our selfhood."[64] James concludes then, that the self is the
given structure of interests in the nature of man. It is in
response to these interests and purposes that consciousness
exerts its selectivity. Because of the immediacy of our practical
needs, the self is generally experienced as muscular movements
of adjustments. This however, does not preclude the existence
of a wider, spiritual self. This self can be described as the
given structure of interests in man's nature and it is *experienced*
in the exercise of our free will. James' account of our awareness
of the activity of free will and a world open to the novelty and
additions produced by the exercise of our free will is the central
concern of *A Pluralistic Universe*.

Radical empiricism: a pluralistic universe

Radical empiricism's general conclusion concerns the structure of the world. James argued that since the experienced world
contains both intimacy and externality, "the directly apprehended universe needs no extraneous trans-empirical support,
but possesses in its own right a concatenated or continuous
structure."[65] James proposes that the world is not in need of an
absolute to make it a *universe*; it is, as it is experienced, a
*pluri*verse. Although his discussion of the former, his polemic
against monistic idealism, is in many ways the central concern
of *A Pluralistic Universe*, our interest is in the latter, his description of the structure of the pluriverse as an alternative world
view.[66] In our first section we will follow James' analysis of
our experience of activity which suggests radical empiricism's
general conclusion. He will argue that in our experiences of
activity we perceptually encounter the effectual causation of
novelty. In the second section, we will discuss monistic idealism's objection that the introduction of novelty renders plural-

ism's world view irrational. There we will also briefly examine James' appraisal of *monism versus pluralism*. Third, if our actions introduce novelty into the world, it is within our power to decide the world's future—James' doctrine of *meliorism*. Finally, we will treat James' position on *a finite God*.

1. *Our experience of activity*. In his presidential address to the American Psychological Association in 1904, James suggests that much confusion concerning our notion of activity could be eliminated if it were pragmatically defined. His treatment is in two stages: a discussion of our perceptual experience of activity and an analysis of the implications of this experience. Initially we are aware of activity as something going on. However our own experience of ourselves as actors allows us to further specify this notion. In these experiences mere going on is specified as change with reference to purposes or ends. Further, this experience is complicated with resistances which our activity succumbs to or overcomes. In these experiences of a change in view of an end, with resistance encountered, argues James, we discover the source of our notion of *causal efficacy*:

> There [in these experiences of overcoming obstacles] is complete activity in its original and first intention. . . . The experiencer of such a situation possesses all that the idea [of causal efficacy] contains. He feels the tendency, the obstacle, the will, the strain, the triumph or the passive giving up, just as he feels the time, the space, swiftness or intensity, the movement, the weight and color, the pain and pleasure.[67]

James submits that in our own experience of activity we encounter the ultimate nature of reality as surely as we do in our experience of "red," "hard," "loud": "the concrete perceptual flux, taken just as it comes, offers in our own activity-situations perfectly comprehensible instances of causal agency."[68] He next asks what difference will it make if we accept the reality of our experiences of causal efficacy.

Acceptance of the reality of our experiences of causal efficacy means, first of all, that our moral experience of impugnability is traceable to a concrete experience. I am responsible for my actions since I am the source of change; in my activities I create new facts: "If we take an activity-situation at its face value, it seems as if we caught *in flagrante delicto* the very power that makes facts come and be."[69] In a word, I am responsible for my activities because I introduce novelty into the world. James holds, then, that an examination of our primal experiences of activity puts us into immediate touch with the fact of novelty in the world:

> Sustaining, persevering, striving, paying with effort as we go, hanging on, and finally achieving our intention—this *is* action, this *is* effectuation in the only shape in which by pure experience-philosophy, the whereabouts of it anywhere can be discussed. Here is creation in its first intention, here is causality at work. . . . I conclude then, that real effectual causation as an ultimate nature, is a "category" if you like, of reality, *is just what we feel it to be*, just that conjunction which our own activity series reveal.[70]

James concludes that our activity-series reveal perfectly comprehensible examples of causal efficacy. In these experiences of causal efficacy we have an acquaintance-knowledge of our moral experience of impugnability and of the fact of novelty in the world. The reality of novelty is the fundamental pragmatic difference between monism and pluralism.

2. *Pluralism versus monism.*   In this section we will summarize James' evaluation of monism and pluralism as world views.

Negatively, he will argue that although monism does indeed give us a unified, completely rational world, that gain is an empty one, for monism solves its theoretical problem by reducing the experiences of the "whole man" to appearances. Positively, he suggests that pluralism's acceptance of the world given in our experience (unfinished, open, growing, changing) is a more rational[71] world view since it is verifiable and since it can accommodate the experiences of the "whole man." Further, he grants that even though the world of pluralism is not a completely unified whole, the introduction of novelty does not yield a completely irrational, chaotic world.

He begins by describing the philosopher's attempt to attain a "total view." he suggests that the search begins in response to the intellect's desire for a unified, rational view of reality. Any total view, he submits, must be based on a model—some particular experience which the philosopher feels most truly to reveal reality. In a distinctive Jamesian fashion he argues that because of temperament, monists and pluralists have chosen different experiences as paradigmatic—pluralists, struck by the particularity of the experienced world, explain wholes in terms of parts, and monists, struck by the interconnectedness of reality, explain parts in terms of wholes. The point of this analysis is not to reduce our choice of world views to temperamental and emotive appeal but to emphasize the subjective factors at work: "All philosophies are *hypotheses*, to which all our faculties, emotional as well as logical, help us."[72] Yet, even though both world views are hypotheses based on subjective factors, "what distinguishes a philosopher's truth is that it is *reasoned*."[73] Accordingly, our criterion for evaluating monism and pluralism will then be *rationality*.

In *Some Problems of Philosophy* James discusses the monist's view that the world is a determined whole. He suggests that this view characterized by oneness and total coimplication of parts seems supremely more rational than the pluralist's world view which allows growth by the introduction of novelty. For the monist, there is a total interdependence of parts so that the alteration of one part involves the alteration of every other part. Further, this total coimplication of parts involves a determined world. However, inasmuch as the idealists construe the absolute (who constitutes the universe and guides its development) religiously, the world's salvation is inevitable. Hence the idealist's monistic, block-world is able to confer religious stability and security. Monism, then, seems rational insofar as it gives us a totally unified world and satisfies our need for assurance.

There are, however, defects in this world view. First, it does not account for our finite minds and their limited knowledge— although all things might exist as the Absolute knows them, our thoughts exist as *we* know them. If the Absolute be the cause of our thoughts, he is the cause of error and ignorance. Second, there is the problem of evil. If the world is a total, perfect unity constituted by an Absolute, why is there evil and how can a perfect Absolute either cause it or allow it? Third, a perfect, finished world contradicts the world as we perceive it—full of change, growth, and becoming. Finally, a determined world is fatalistic. In it, since the future is totally implicated with the past, our experiences of freedom and responsibility are derealized. In short, monism's view of the world is defective in that it reduces most of our significant human experiences to the level of appearance.

Pluralism's view of the world treats these same experiences as real. In a pluralistic world:

> the common-sense view of life, as something really dramatic with work to be done and things decided here and now, is acceptable to pluralism. "Free will" means nothing but real novelty; so pluralism accepts the notion of free will.[74]

Although pluralism accepts our experiences of freedom and novelty, it is unable to offer monism's religious peace and security, for in a pluralistic world, our actions decide the world's future. Pluralism does however have the following advantages. First, it is more empirical for it accepts the world as we experience it—characterized by both externality and intimacy. Monism, on the other hand, accepts only conjunctive relations, yet "to make the conjunctions more vital and primordial than separations, monism has to abandon verifiable experiences and proclaim a unity that is indescribable."[75] Second, pluralism agrees with the experience of the "whole man" that real work is to be done and that our free actions actually contribute to the direction the world's future takes. Third, pluralism is more defensible for "it is not obliged to stand for any amount of plurality, for it triumphs over monism if the smallest morsel of disconnectedness is once found undeniably to exist."[76] Pluralism, then, seems more rational insofar as it agrees with our perceptual experience of the world and our moral experiences.

Which account is more reasonable? Monism obviously gives us a rational, unified world view. *Too* rational and *too* unified, answers James. He argues that monism has only satisfied the intellect's demands for unity; whereas there are three other demands which must be satisfied in order to have true rationality:

> Men are once for all so made that they prefer a rational world to believe in and to live in. But rationality has at least four dimensions, intellectual, aesthetic, moral and practical; and to find a world rational to the maximal degree *in all these respects simultaneously* is no easy matter. . . . The rationality we gain in one coin, we thus pay for in another; and the problem accordingly seems . . . to resolve

itself into that of getting a conception which will yield the largest *balance* of rationality.[77]

Monism has respected only the intellect's demand for unity and in the process it has had to neglect the other dimensions of rationality. Pluralism, argues James, gives a better account of all the demands of rationality. A pluralistic view accepts as real our perceptual experience of the world—it is this experience which guides the satisfaction of our most basic, survival-orientated needs. Pluralism views the world as only a partially unified whole, hence it can account for our moral experiences of freedom and impugnability. Since our actions are not coimplicated with the past, our experiences of activity can be taken at their face value—I am responsible for my actions for by them I introduce novelty into the world. Finally, since the world is not finished and perfect, evil is not a speculative problem; it is a concrete problem awaiting the proper use of human freedom.

To summarize, James proposes that the monism/pluralism option should be judged according to the criterion of true rationality. He has argued that true rationality is attained when a variety of demands is satisfied. Since pluralism meets those demands more adequately, it gives us a more rational view of the world. Negatively monism's postulation of total unity is useless for deductive purposes—"you cannot enter the phenomenal world with the notion of it [total unity] in your grasp and name beforehand any detail which you are likely to meet there,"[78] hence it can never be a practical, problem-solving philosophy. In fact, monism, in order to solve the problem of human error is forced to brand our perceptual access to particulars, and our awareness of the temporal, changing character of reality as an illusion. Further, monism's desire for total unity necessitates its relegating our moral experiences to the level of appearance. Positively, pluralism accepts our perceptual experience of the world and the world as we experience it.

Since the world is open and unfinished our moral experiences can be accepted as real. Because our free actions introduce novelty into the world and thereby determine its future course, the human agent is put in a privileged position. In a pluralistic world, reality is, in a very real way, shaped by man. Before we turn to this melioristic world which man may shape, we must treat one objection to pluralism.

Doesn't the introduction of novelty lead to chaos and ultimately render pluralism an irrational world view? James responds that this charge only holds if you accept the disjunction: either total rationality or total irrationality. He proposes that since the idealists are able to perceive only disjunction in the world, they feel it necessary to import extra-experiential connective support in order to attain a unified world. In this totally unified, block-world, novelties would indeed be an irrational, chaotic factor. However, radical empiricism holds that conjunctive relations are experienced and are real, hence extra-experiential connective support is unnecessary. The perceived world contains both conjunctions and disjunctions:

> May not the flux of sensible experience itself contain a rationality that has been overlooked, so that the real remedy would consist in harking back to *it* (sensible experience) more intelligently and not in advancing in the opposite direction away from it . . . to that pseudorationality of the supposed absolute point of view.[79]

James suggests that the world already contains a unity, a connectedness, a rationality; and this rationality pluralism accepts:

> *Some* rationality certainly does characterize our universe; and, weighing one kind with another, we may deem that the incomplete kinds that appear are, on the whole as

acceptable as the through-and-through sort of rationality on which the monistic systematizers insist.[80]

In this partially unified world, novelty will not appear suddenly, *ex nihilo*, but it will develop gradually within experience, "novelty, as empirically found, doesn't arrive by jumps and jolts, it leaks in insensibly, for adjacents in experience are always interfused."[81] In our own experience of activity, we experience the introduction of novelty and it is only from an analysis of these experiences that we can discover the genuine changing, temporal, open-ended character of reality. "To an observer standing outside of its generating-causes, novelty can only appear as so much 'chance,' to one who stands inside it, it is the expression of 'free creative activity.' "[82] It is now apparent how radically James' philosophy is a humanism. He holds that not only does the human element pervade all of our thinking and "filter" reality's corrective pressure, but the inner-most nature of *reality itself* is experienced in and through human activities. We will return to this in our concluding chapter.

3. *A melioristic universe.* Though meliorism is a central con-cept in *A Pluralistic Universe*, James' most systematic expression of this doctrine is in the last chapter of *Pragmatism*, "Pragma-tism and Religion." A little reflection will show the intimate connection between meliorism and religion. In our above dis-cussion, we have seen James' position on the rationality of monism. Throughout the discussion, monism's satisfaction of man's religious desire for peace and security was considered a plus in its favor. On the other hand, pluralism was discussed chiefly in terms of its satisfaction of man's ethical desires. At first sight, it appears that pluralism fails to satisfy man's religious demands. This then is the context of James' discussion of meliorism—pluralism's relation to man's religious desires.

In a monistic world, the future is determined; the world's salvation[83] is either impossible or inevitable. The idealistic monism James opposes holds that the absolute who directs the world's future renders its salvation inevitable. In a pluralistic world, since our experience of novelty is accepted as real, our own actions determine the world's future:

> Our acts, our turning-places, where we seem to ourselves to make ourselves and grow, are the parts of the world to which we are closest, the parts of which our knowledge is most intimate and complete. Why should we not take them at their face-value? Why may they not be the actual turning-places and growing-places which they seem to be, of the world—why not the workshop of being, where we catch fact in the making, so that nowhere may the world grow in any other way than this.[84]

James here reaffirms the point made above. We are most intimately acquainted with our own activity and, in that activity, we experience the introduction of novelty. If we take our experience at face value, then the world's future is, at least in part, determined by our own actions. The monists charge that this means the introduction of novelty at various points, by a variety of agents, without any overall plan or without any reference to total design. Only if the agent be the integral whole, can the development of the world be logically explained, they insist. James replies that novelty from independent agents without reference to a preconceived plan is, in fact, the way we experience our own activity. He submits that the point is the world we experience grows "piecemeal by the contribution of its several parts."[85] But if there is no overall plan, the salvation of the world isn't assured. Granted, answers James. But isn't this the way we experience the world? Suppose the author of the world put this case to you, at the moment of creation:

> I am going to make a world not certain to be saved, a world the perfection of which shall be conditioned merely, the

condition being that each several agent does its own "level best." I offer you the chance of taking part in such a world. Its safety, you see, is unwarranted. It is a real adventure, with real danger, yet it may win through. It is a social scheme of co-operative work genuinely to be done. Will you join the procession? Will you trust yourself and trust the other agents enough to face the risk?[86]

In this world there is real risk, real error, real loss and real triumph. This melioristic world is the world as we experience it; none of our experiences need be de-realized. In this world, the human contribution is paramount; indeed, it is the ultimate determinant of the world's future. In this world human freedom is real—its exercise actually determines the world's outcome. In this world, salvation is neither impossible nor inevitable; it is possible, it must be won by man. We will return to this thoroughgoing humanism in the last chapter.

In direct answer to the objection that his melioristic world view does not satisfy man's religious desires, James refers to a distinction made in *The Varieties of Religious Experience*. There he suggested that there are two kinds of religion: the religion of the healthy-minded, "self-sufficingness" and, the religion of the sick-souled, "self-surrender."[87] Once again we see James employing a variation of his "tough- and tender-minded" categories. Here it seems that there is a genuine will-to-believe option. Yet one of the conditions of the will to believe is that we may choose the option which agrees with our passional nature, *provided all things are equal*. But in this case, all things are not equal between monism and pluralism. James argues to choose a monistic, determined world because it agrees with our religious desire for peace and security is tantamount to choosing monism because it satisfies the intellect's demand for complete unity. In the process of satisfying our "sick-souled" religious demands, monism's determined world relegates our experiences of freedom, risk, good, and bad to appearance. He submits that in order to preserve the reality of those experiences, we must accept the risk of an open, undetermined world, in which there is real loss and real gain. If we face a life of un-certified possibilities, the highest exercise of our powers is demanded, and, concludes James, it is in the exercise of these powers that we experience the human way of being to the limit. Yet in this melioristic universe there is still a place for God and to this final aspect of James' pluralistic universe we now turn.

4. *A finite God.*   Even though the course of the world's future is dependent upon our efforts, ours are not the only efforts. A coworker in this shaping of the world's outcome is God—"one helper, *primus inter pares*, in the midst of all the shapers of the great world's fate."[88] In *The Will to Believe* and *The Varieties of Religious Experience*, James argues that belief in God is warranted insofar as it satisfies our needs and produces in us real effects. Chief of these real effects is an increase in moral energy creating an added willingness to adopt the strenuous mood. The strenu-ous mood expresses itself by working to change the status quo in order to bring the largest amount of good into existence. In the previous section, James suggested that the world's salvation is possible, "the condition being that each of several agents does his 'level best,' "[89] that is, adopts the strenuous mood.[90] Hence, in James' thought from a variety of angles, belief in God is pragmatically warranted. What can we say of the nature of God?

James has argued that if the metaphysical problem of evil is to be obviated the world cannot be whole and perfect; hence God must be finite:

The line of least resistance, as it seems to me, both in theology and in philosophy, is to accept . . . that there is a

God, but that he is finite, either in power or in knowledge, or in both at once.[91]

Not only does a finite God eliminate the metaphysical problem of evil, a finite God corresponds more closely with our religious experiences of him. In these experiences, God is practically involved in our lives, "having an environment, being in time, and working out a history just like ourselves, he escapes from all the foreignness . . . of the static, timeless, perfect absolute (of idealistic monism)."[92] God as a finite, coworker, observes James, far different from the transcendent, detached being of traditional theism, can truly make a real difference in the conduct of our lives:

> "God" in the religious lives of ordinary men, is the name, not of the whole of things, heaven forbid, but only of the ideal tendency in things, believed in as a superhuman person who calls us to co-operate in his purposes, and who furthers ours if they are worthy. He works in an external environment, has limits, and has enemies.[93]

James observes that a finite God not only obviates theoretical difficulties but since he affords the highest degree of intimacy, he also makes the greatest practical difference and most strongly encourages the strenuous mood. God, then, is a personal being with whom men may commune so that as coworker, they share the same tasks, aiding each other. Yet this finite God of a melioristic universe appeals not only to the "healthy-minded." Though finite, he is the first among finite things. He offers security and peace in answer to our "sick-souled" needs, for he guarantees the permanent preservation of an ideal moral order:

> The world may indeed, as science assures us, some day burn up or freeze; but if it is part of his order, the old ideals are

sure to be brought elsewhere to fruition, so that where God is tragedy is only provisional and partial, and shipwreck and dissolution are not the absolutely final things.[94]

Nevertheless this assurance that a permanent moral order will be preserved does not remove us from the task of making that moral order concrete. In the end, belief in God practically changes the world through our actions. Though belief in God may indeed encourage us to adopt the strenuous mood, it is *our* efforts that will make the world's salvation an actuality. Once again James affirms his stand on the importance of human action. James' pluralistic universe is an arena in which the exercise of man's freedom determines the outcome of the world; in such a world man is raised to a new dignity and importance.

In this chapter, we have seen James' mature philosophical thought in relation to his theory of man. We have proposed that James' theory of man provides the proper theme for understanding and unifying his thought. In this chapter we have shown that his mature philosophical positions are explications and justifications of previous stands on the nature of man.

For example, not only did James employ the pragmatic theory of meaning in his early investigations in psychology, ethics, and religion, but the philosophical foundation for that theory is his stand on the instrumental character of human knowledge. Further, James' distinctive interpretation of the pragmatic theory of meaning holds that concepts can be pragmatically defined in terms of particular aesthetic, ethical, and religious experiences. In short, his pragmatic theory of meaning is worked out with a view to accommodating the experiences of the "whole man." In his pragmatic theory of truth, James argued that true ideas "successfully lead." "Successful leading," he contends, can only be judged in terms of the satisfactoriness of terminal experiences. Since "satisfactoriness" can only be evaluated in terms of the concrete contribution of interests and purposes (which initiated the inquiry) the human contribution intrudes into all our dealings with reality. Hence, James' theory of truth is an articulation of his mature humanism—all truths are human products made within the tissue of human experience. James' account of how ideas lead within experience and his description of a world malleable enough to tolerate the human addition is expressed in his doctrine of radical empiricism.

In his *Essays in Radical Empiricism*, James works out an epistemology consonant with the instrumental character of human knowing. He argues that in our concrete experiences of the knowledge-relation, ideas do not *represent*, rather they *lead us* within experience in order to put us into "working touch" with reality. He suggests that if reality be considered "pure experience," it can function both as the knower and as the known. Hence, we can avoid the traditional problem of the "gap," since in perceptual knowledge the thing known and the knowing of it are really an identical "bit" of pure experience considered from two different contexts. Conceptual knowledge, proposes James, can also be explained as a relation within experience—ideas function by guiding us through a series of intermediaries (provided by a mental or physical context) towards or into direct contact with reality. This account of knowing, concludes James, without resorting to extra-experiential mechanism, is able to explain knowing as it is experienced— a conjunctive, "ambulatory" relation within experience.

In *A Pluralistic Universe*, James describes a world consonant with the experiences of the "whole man." He begins with an analysis of our experience of activity. From this analysis he concludes that in these experiences of ourselves as actors we encounter the introduction of novelty into the world. A world which can admit the introduction of novelty cannot be a completely unified totality. Granted, says James, but do we not experience precisely such a world: partially unified, growing, and changing? James concludes that a pluralistic view of the world is not forced to de-realize (as monism must) either our perceptual knowledge or our experiences of freedom, novelty, and impugnability. Instead, in such a world the experiences of the "whole man" are dignified, for the exercise of human freedom determines the future of an undetermined world. In his description of a pluralistic, melioristic world, James once again articulates his philosophy in terms of man. From a variety of angles and in a variety of ways, then, James' philosophy is a humanism. In our final chapter we will discuss the unifying ramifications of this theme of humanism in the thought of William James.

5

"Humanism" as a unifying theme in James' philosophy

In this final chapter, we will draw together the various strands of James' philosophy of man and discuss the unifying ramifications of the theme of humanism in his thought. In the first section we will retrace the main lines of his theory of man as it developed from his psychology, through his ethical and religious thought and its place in his mature metaphysics and epistemology. Special attention will be given to his struggle with the problem of the self and its resolution in his mature thought which allowed him to accept, without reservation, an interactionist view of man in which consciousness is efficacious by selection. In the second section we will discuss the various facets of James' humanism. There we will argue that James' central concern with man led him from his own technical use of the term "humanism" (as a theory of truth, based on his position on the nature of human experience) to an articulation of humanism in the classical sense—that man is the center of the whole of things.

JAMES' THEORY OF MAN

James begins his psychological study of man by proposing that psychology be an empirical, scientific study of the phe-

163

nomena of mental life (characterized by him as "The pursuance of future ends and the choice of means for their attainment"[1]). However, at the outset he argues that if our experience that thoughts and feelings (generally, he uses the term "consciousness") influence our behavior is to be accepted as genuine, consciousness must be efficacious. The efficacy of consciousness is not only consonant with our experience of positing ends and guiding activity in view of those ends but also with the moral and religious experiences of the "whole man." Hence James offers as a hypothesis an interactionist view of man in which consciousness is efficacious. It is important to notice that in his psychology James does not use the experiences of the "whole man" to argue that such a view of man *must* be the case; instead he uses these experiences to propose a hypothesis which is then checked against the data of introspection. If he were to simply frame a view of man using man's moral and religious desires he could have simply concluded that consciousness is efficacious through the agency of a substantial soul which initiates activities. Instead James argues that all that is given in introspection is that consciousness is (among other things)[2] personal and that it is selective. Nevertheless he submits that these characteristics warrant a provisional acceptance of the efficacy of consciousness, and hence an interactionist view of man.

He argues that in all its forms, from sensation to voluntary action, consciousness exhibits selectivity. Consciousness does not passively reflect reality but it is active and interested, functioning for the satisfaction of the needs and purposes of the organism. He concludes that consciousness is by its very nature impulsive: "It is of the essence of all consciousness to instigate movement of some sort."[3] If a self, an I as thinker, would also be discovered among the data of introspection, the efficacy of consciousness would be confirmed. That is, the self as the agent of selection would simply have to attend to one idea (while suppressing that idea's opposite) and movement would occur since conscious states "naturally" instigate movement.[4] This is, in fact, submits James, the way the higher states of consciousness are efficacious in directing behavior. He proposes that *attention* in the stream of consciousness is the mechanism of the self's selection and that the interests and purposes of the self control the fixing of attention. Unforunately, such a substantial self as thinker and agent of selection is not empirically given. James observes that all that is given is "passing thought" and since "passing thought" can functionally account for both knowing and personal identity there is no warrant for positing a substantial soul.

From his psychology then, James argues that the data of introspection do not wholly substantiate an interactionist view of man in which consciousness is efficacious. However, he continues to provisionally accept the existence of the self (since the self is required by the demands of the "whole man"), and he argues that the empirically given selectivity of consciousness, controlled by the interests and purposes of the self, operating by the mechanism of attention, does support the efficacy of consciousness and hence an interactionist view of man. However, until James resolves the problem of the existence of the self in *A Pluralistic Universe*, this view of man can only be provisionally accepted.

In our third chapter we examined James' account of the ethical and religious experiences of the "whole man." He argued that if these experiences are to be accepted as genuine, certain things about man and the world are requisite. He concludes that his analysis of these experiences will give added support to his previous stand on an interactionist view of man, providing these experiences can be explained in terms of what is empirically given—the selectivity of consciousness.

In his analysis of our moral experiences of freedom and inpugnability, he argues that three conditions are requisite: that man possess true freedom, that man's free acts introduce novelty into the world, and that a world susceptible to these novel additions must be open, unfinished, and undetermined. Hence, his interactionist view of man is further specified—he holds not only that conscious states guide behavior, but, in addition, that man is able to control the stream of his thought. In other words, man is responsible for his behavior for he can control his thoughts which in turn control his actions; therefore, man is free. James also maintains that the empirically given selectivity of consciousness can account for our experiences of free choice since the feeling of effort attendant to responsibly choosing can be explained in terms of the mental effort exerted in sustaining attention to an idea. Notice that he claims that volition is "primarily a relation, not between our self and extramental matter, but between our self and our own states of mind."[5] Even though his analysis of ethical experiences further supports his interactionist view of man, and even though "selective attention" is able to provide a satisfactory psychological explanation for our experience of responsible choice, his commitment to that view of man remains provisional since he has not yet resolved the question of the existence of the self.

Further, he suggests that ethical interests and purposes (moral ideals) provide the control for the *fixing of attention* in our free choices. He argues that these moral ideals are not simply given structures in man's nature but that they are sentiments of felt fitness which are generated by an interplay between given structures in man's nature and "front- and back-door" experiences. Though the mechanism of this interplay remains unclear, it is important, for it is an attempt on James' part to explain the diversity among individuals' moral ideals. Unfortunately, notes James, the uniqueness of these diverse moral ideals is not often expressed for most men do not adopt the "strenuous mood" but instead acquiesce to society's existing moral code by adopting the "genial mood." James turns to religious experience for a solution to this difficulty. He maintains that religious experience encourages the adoption of the "strenuous mood," and moreover, since religion promotes a respect for the uniqueness of individuals, it provides us with a paradigm for an ideal society—characterized by the fullest possible expression of every one's unique moral sensibilities. In his examination of man's ethical experiences, then, James finds additional support for an interactionist view of man, now further specified by a commitment to man's freedom, and he maintains that the empirically given selectivity of consciousness can account for these experiences.

James begins his analysis of religious experiences with an examination of the nature and legitimacy of belief. He argues that belief is but another human activity which can be explained by consciousness's selectivity, and he describes it as a conscious state akin to an emotion characterized by a willingness to act. Our beliefs, controlled by our desires and interests, prompt actions. These actions correct our beliefs in terms of successful or abortive interaction with the world. He concludes that the criteria available to us in belief decisions are the demands of our passional nature and the corrective character of experience. However, in certain cases, our actions do not so much correct our initial beliefs as actually create their own verification. In these cases, we have the right to believe according to the desires and interests of our passional natures, for a refusal to believe involves a failure to act and therein a failure to create the verification for the initial belief. James concludes that his analysis of belief has indicated yet another instance of the selectivity of human experience. Further, his analysis of our belief in various worlds (e.g., common sense, scientific theories, philosophies(indicates to what extent our desires and interests control our *selection* of these worlds.

In his attempts to offer psychological explanations for the varieties of religious experience, James finds himself expanding his notion of "human." For example, he explains religious conversion as a shifting of attention to a new center of desires and interests. Even sudden conversion, he suggests, can be explained as the replacement of the normal self by an active and well developed subliminal self. Conversion, then, can be explained in terms of a new set of ideas and interests controlling consciousness's selectivity, and hence governing the behavior of the converted believer. However, the real importance of James' psychological explanation of conversion is that he now begins to think of the self as a *structure of interests* and he begins to realize that the self is experienced in terms of other interests besides the survival-orientated ones—which are experienced as cephalic movements of adjustment.

James' analysis of sainthood also expands his notion of "human." He suggests that if the normal, practical criterion (adjustment to existing society) is used to evaluate the ethical excellence of a saint, the meaning of that religious experience is compromised. James maintains that sainthood must be evaluated in terms of the unseen world. He concludes that even though mysticism (and also natural theology) is unable to provide an objective warrant for the existence of the unseen world, we nevertheless have a right to believe in that world. Belief in God and in the unseen world is justified, argues James, since that belief satisfies the needs and desires of the believer and that world is real at least insofar as it produces real effects in the believer. However, James' analysis of mysticism is important for his theory of man since it expands his notion of "human" and thereby provides a solution for the existence of the self. He argued, "the existence of mystical states absolutely overthrows the pretention of nonmystical states to be the sole and ultimate dictators of what we may believe."[6] Further, his psychological explanation of mystical states—that the mystic is able to contact the higher power because his real self is coterminous with that higher power—gave him added confidence in the existence of a wider self.

In our fourth chapter we discussed James' mature thought in relation to his theory of man. There we saw that his pragmatic theory of meaning was based on his position on the instrumental character of human knowledge. He argued that ideas, as guides to future actions, mean the concrete consequences they lead us to. This theory of meaning is consonant with the experiences of the "whole man" for he held that particular ethical and religious experiences can pragmatically define a concept. As a theory of truth, James argued that true ideas successfully lead and that "successful leading" can only be evaluated with reference to the purposes and interests which originally initiated the inquiry. He suggested that since human interests and purposes not only initiate inquiry but are employed to evaluate the success of an idea's leading function, truths are "man-made." (We will continue this in our final section.) James' account of how ideas lead and his description of a world open to man-made truths is expressed in his doctrine of radical empiricism.

Although the central concern of James' radical empiricism is his position on the knowledge-relation as an experienced, ambulatory, conjunctive relation, our interest in this overview on his theory of man is in his resolution of the problem of the existence of the self. He begins his radical empiricism by stating that he will observe the postulate that only things experienced are to be considered real. As we have seen, even though he felt that the existence of the self was required by man's ethical religious experiences, he maintained that the self was only *experienced* as cephalic movements of adjustment. James now proposed that this self, experienced as muscular adjustment, was only a portion of a wider self. Moreover, the wider self was itself experienced in ethical and religious experiences wherein the wider self moves from the periphery (subconscious awareness) to the center (conscious awareness). (Notice that this explanation uses precisely the same model as his account of conversion.) In short, James argues that not only is the self requisite for the experiences of the "whole man" but that this "full self" is itself actually *experienced* in the exercise of free will. The self can be described as the structure of interests which control consciousness's selectivity, and the self is experienced as the source of our feelings of spontaneous psychic effort, i.e., the source of our ability to resolutely sustain attention to an idea. James is now finally able to adopt, without reservation,[7] the interactionist view of man in which consciousness is efficacious. Consciousness is efficacious by selection, *controlled* by a structure of interests and purposes, *through the agency of a self* which is experienced as the source of "selective attention."

In *A Pluralistic Universe*, James describes the kind of world which can accommodate the experiences of the "whole man." He argues that an unfinished, undetermined, open world is not only consonant with the religious and ethical aspirations of man, but that it is also the kind of world we experience. He proposes, for example, that in our experiences of activity, we have immediate acquaintance with the introduction of novelty into the world; moreover, a world open to novel additions is a world which can accommodate our moral experiences—freedom, risk, triumph and loss, good and evil. In such a melioristic world, the world's salvation is neither inevitable nor impossible; it is only possible—dependent on the proper exercise of human freedom. In this melioristic world, God is conceived to be a finite, coworker. A finite God, argues James, corresponds with the God of religious experience, and since he is finite, the metaphysical problem of evil is obviated.

In his mature thought then, James worked out a metaphysics and an epistemology which were both consonant with the aspirations of the "whole man" and at the same time, true to our experiences of the knowledge-relation, our experience of activity, and our perceptual experience of the world. There he also finally resolved the problem of the existence of the self as agent, which up to then had forced him to only provisionally accept an interactionist view of man. Notice that even though throughout his thought James used the aspirations of the "whole man" to *suggest* hypotheses concerning man and the world, he did not accept those hypotheses unless they were borne out by experience. This difficult loyalty both to preconception and experienced facts capsulizes the subtlety and insightfulness of James' pragmatic humanism.

As we have noted, James felt the sway of "tough- and tender-minded" demands in his thought. He specifically invisioned his pragmatism as a *media via* between those two tendencies. His goal was to be objective (which he describes as strict adherence to experienced fact) without compromising or de-realizing man's moral and religious aspiration. That James did not simply capitulate to the "tender-minded" demands of the "whole man" has been detailed in the long struggle with the question of the existence of a substantial self. His acceptance of that self, and, in turn, his acceptance of an interactionist view of man, remained tentative and provisional until he could justify the existence of the self with reference to a particular, concrete experience of it. On the other hand, despite his life-long preoccupation with psychical research, he concluded that the experienced facts did not provide sufficient evidence for a substantial, personal soul. Hence, James' presuppositions not-withstanding, the cutting edge of strict adherence to experienced fact is felt in his theory of man. Yet has he not also continually pointed out that all experience bears the imprint of human interests and purposes? Has he not maintained that the corrective pressure of reality is only felt through the filter of human experience? In short, has he not concluded that the human contribution intrudes into all our thinking to such an extent that all our truths are man-made? He refers to this position on the nature of human experience and the nature of truth as "humanism." To that theme in his thought we now turn.

JAMES' PHILOSOPHY AS A "HUMANISM"

In a variety of interrelated ways, James' philosophy is a humanism. In this final section, we will both delineate the various facets of his humanism and show how his overriding concern with the nature of man leads him from his own technical use of that term to an affirmation of classical humanism—man is the center of the whole of things.

The "whole man" as a guide to inquiry

Throughout his thought James uses the demands of the "whole man" to guide his investigations. We have seen, for example, that in his psychology he proposes that if the ethical and religious experiences of man are to be accepted as genuine, an interactionist view of man is required. Or, from the same experiences, in his metaphysics, he suggests that the world must be unfinished, open, and undetermined. Hence, the demands of the "whole man" are used by James to frame hypotheses. It is important to notice that his procedure is not to argue that man's ethical and religious aspirations dictate that such and such must necessarily be the case; instead he uses those aspirations to suggest hypotheses which are then checked against experience. His position on the nature of human experience provides us with the second facet of his "humanism."

James' theory of truth as a "humanism"

From his analysis of human experience, James concludes that the above-mentioned model of inquiry—a tentative hypothesis, checked against experience—proves to be oversimplified. He argues that the demands of the "whole man" which suggest the original hypothesis do, in fact, influence the very experiences which are supposed to confirm or correct the initial hypothesis. James maintains that the human access to reality is not passive and disinterested; instead, all forms of consciousness are active and interested. In other words, human interests and purposes pervade all our thinking—"to an unascertainable extent all our truths are man-made products. Human motives sharpen all our questions, human satisfactions lurk in all our answers, all our formulas have a human twist."[8] He observes that the human element in our thinking is so unavoidable that our conceptions "characterize *us* more than they characterize the thing."[9] In short, human experience is theory-laden; we cannot encounter reality-in-itself; for our consciousness, in response to needs and purposes presents only a *selection* of aspects. He concludes, "You can't weed out the human contribution."[10] Yet even though, "all our truths . . . are affected by race-inheritance with a human coefficient,"[11] we need not conclude that the human contribution constitutes a distortion of the real. Such a conclusion, suggests James, follows only if man and the world are artificially separated.

Human experiences as revelatory of the nature of reality

The inability of human experiences to be objective (i.e., neutrally disinterested) does not preclude our knowing the *real*, for man and his activities are part and parcel of reality. James suggests, for example, that our moral experiences of freedom and impugnability lead us to suppose that the world is susceptible to novel additions. But, is this not the very world given in our experience? In fact, do we not directly encounter in our own experiences of activity ourselves introducing novelty into the world—"are [we] not here witnessing in our own personal experience what is really the essential process of creation? Is not the world really growing in these activities of ours?"[12] Moreover, James maintains that novelty can be properly understood only from within, from the perspective of the actor. Hence, an examination of our own experiences of novelty provides the proper access to ascertaining the actual character of the world—undetermined, unfinished, and open to novelty. James is openly and admittedly anthropomorphic. He suggests, first of all, that since we are most intimately acquainted with our own experiences, these experiences should guide our understanding of the world. Further, he argues that since man is a part of the world, his experiences of activity are not simply reliable guides to the nature of the world, but that in these experiences we have immediate acquaintance with the world as it is. That is, through the exercise of human freedom the world is actually being determined through the novel additions of man. James then holds that an analysis of human experiences (especially the experience of activity) reveals the nature of reality. This conclusion leads directly to James' position on the nature of philosophy.

Philosophy as an articulation of the human perspective

Since the interests and purposes of man not only guide inquiry and fund our experience but also since our experience of ourselves reveals the very nature of the world, philosophy can but be an expression of the human way of being. "A philosophy is the expression of a man's intimate character, and all definitions of the universe are but the deliberately adopted reactions of human characters upon it."[13] James argues that the search for a totally disinterested, objective view is both futile and impossible. Since the human contribution intrudes into all our thinking, all we can hope to attain in a philosophy is the most adequate human perspective. That perspective, argues

James, will be the one which exhibits true rationality—i.e., satisfies all the demands (practical, intellectual, aesthetic, ethical, and religious) which constitute the sentiment of rationality. He maintains, for example, that monism's deterministic, block-view of the world only satisfies the intellect's demand for unity. The other demands of rationality are neglected by monism, for it is forced to relegate man's practical and moral experience to the level of appearance. He submits that his melioristic, pluralistic philosophy is more adequate, for it is not forced to *de-realize* either the experiences of the "whole man" or our perceptual experience of the world. His philosophy, he argues, is truly a human philosophy because it finds rationality without resorting to extra-experiential sources:

> Humanism is willing to let finite experiences be self supporting. . . . The essential service of humanism . . . is to have seen that tho one part of our experience may lean upon another part to make it what it is in any one of several aspects in which it may be considered, experience as a whole is self-containing and hangs on nothing.[14]

Besides letting human experiences be self-supporting, James' melioristic philosophy constitutes the most adequate human philosophy, for it puts man in a truly central position.

The dignity of man in James' philosophy

James argues that his melioristic, pluralistic philosophy dignifies man, for man is responsible for the world his actions create. He maintains that not only is his melioristic view of the world consonant with man's moral and religious experiences but it is, in fact, the world we experience:

> In our cognitive as well as in our active life we are creative.

We *add*, both to the subject and to the predicate parts of reality. The world stands really malleable, waiting to receive its final touches at our hands.[15]

In such a world, both man's philosophy and his activities are momentous parts of reality.

Man's philosophy, argues James, "is itself an intimate part of the universe, and it may be a part momentous enough to give a different turn to what the other parts signify."[16] If the world is, as we experience it, unfinished and open to the human contribution, our adoption of a philosophy which not only holds that men are free but urges the full use of that freedom, will indeed change the shape of reality:

This is the philosophy of humanism in the widest sense. Our philosophies swell the current of being, add their character to it. They are part of all that we have met, all that makes us be. As a French philosopher says, "Nous sommes du réel dans le réel." Our thoughts determine our acts, and our acts redetermine the previous nature of the world.[17]

Since, in James' view, beliefs lead to action, our belief in the plasticity of the world and in the importance of human actions finds its verification in the actions consequent upon that belief.

James illustrates his position on the centrality of man and his actions in the following way. We normally think that reality is ready-made and complete and our minds simply reflect what is "out there." He suggests the opposite may be true: "may not previous reality itself be there, far less for the purpose of reappearing unaltered in our knowledge, than for the very purpose of stimulating our minds to such additions as shall enhance the universe's total value?"[18] Given this relationship between man and reality, the human contribution is central for it determines the fate of the world. Such a world view, suggests James, is the most adequate human philosophy for it satisfies man's practical, moral, and religious demands, it urges the fullest possible exercise of man's powers, and it places man in the center of things. In this view, man is not simply one of the parts of reality; he is a most momentous part:

> Investigation shows that, in the function called truth, previous realities are not the only independent variables. To a certain extent our ideas, being realities, are also independent variables, and, just as they follow other reality and fit it, so, in a measure, does other reality follow and fit them. When they add themselves to being, they partly redetermine the existent, so that reality as a whole appears incompletely definable unless ideas also are kept account of. *This pragmatist doctrine, exhibiting our ideas as complemental factors of reality, throws open (since our ideas are instigators of our action) a wide window upon human action, as well as a wide licence to originality in thought.* [19]

James concludes that not only is an "objective" (i.e., non-humanistic) total view of reality impossible (given the nature of human experience), but it would be an inadequate view of reality for it would omit the human contribution. [20] He argues that not only are man and his activities part of reality, but that because of the presence of man "some of the realities that he declares true are created by his being there." [21] A view of the world which did not give an account of man and the difference he makes, would omit part of the real—to James' mind the most important part of the real.

James' philosophy is, we submit, a humanism. The central concern of his thought is man. He began his career with a psychological study of man. He then turned to an analysis of the ethical and religious experiences of the "whole man." In the first of his mature works he applies the term "humanism" to his pragmatism. There he argues that ideas can be pragmatically defined in terms of concrete human experiences, be they practical, ethical, or religious. Further, he argues that since all human experience is funded with human purposes and desires, all our truths are man-made. Yet he suggests that the human contribution need not constitute a distortion of reality, for man is a part of reality, and, in fact, through his experiences, man directly encounters the nature of reality. Through his analysis of man's experiences of freedom and activity, he concludes that the world is open, unfinished, and undetermined and that in such a world the activities of man are of paramount importance, for those activities determine the future of the world.

Hence from an analysis of man and human experience, James frames his own humanism as a theory of truth. Further, he argues, a view of the world true to human experience and consonant with the desires of the whole man dignifies man's place in the world. James then moves from a technical and esoteric use of the term "humanism" to the classical sense of that term.[22] Notice, for instance, how similarly the Florentine humanist, Giannozzo Manetti (1396–1459) and James articulate the centrality of man. First, Manetti, in *De Dignitate Hominis*:

> Just as the force, reason, and the power of man, for whom the world itself and all the things of the world were created, are great, straight and admirable, so we must judge and believe that the mission of man consists in knowing and ruling over the world made for him, as well as over all things which we see established in this immense universe.[23]

Now James, in *Pragmatism*:

> The world stands really malleable, waiting to receive its final touches at our hands. Like the kingdom of heaven, it

suffers human violence willingly. Man *engenders* truth upon it. No one can deny that such a role would add to our dignity and to our responsibility as thinkers.[24]

It is our contention that the theme of humanism is the driving force and unifying issue in James' thought. His thought begins and ends with man, and humanism functions efficiently and teleologically to unify and integrate his philosophy.

List of abbreviations

WORKS OF WILLIAM JAMES

CER   *Collected Essays and Review*. New York: Longmans, Green and Co., 1920.

ERE   *Essays in Radical Empiricism*. New York: Longmans, Green and Co., 1912.

MS   *Memories and Studies*. New York: Longmans, Green and Co., 1917.

MT   *The Meaning of Truth, A Sequel to Pragmatism*. New York: Longmans, Green and Co., 1928.

PP   *The Principles of Psychology*. 2 vols. New York: Dover Publications, 1950.

PSY   *Psychology, the Briefer Course*. New York: Henry Holt and Co., 1895.

Prag.   *Pragmatism, and four essays from The Meaning of Truth*. Cleveland: Meridian Books, 1963.

PU   *A Pluralistic Universe: Hibbert Lectures on the Present Situation in Philosophy*. New York: Longmans, Green and Co., 1932.

SPP   *Some Problems of Philosophy*. New York: Longmans, Green and Co., 1931.

VRE *The Varieties of Religious Experience.* New York: Mentor
   Books, 1961.
WB *The Will to Believe and Other Essays on Popular Philosophy.*
   New York: Dover Publications, 1956.

WORKS RELATING TO WILLIAM JAMES

TC Perry, Ralph Barton. *The Thought and Character of William James.* 2 vols. Boston: Little, Brown and Co.,
   1935.
LWJ James, Henry, ed. *The Letters of William James.* 2 vols.
   Boston: The Atlantic Monthly Press, 1920.

Notes

Chapter 1

1. "Review of F.C.S. Schiller's *Humanism*," *Nation* 78 (1904): 175-76, reprinted in *CER*, pp. 450-51.
2. *Prag.*, p. 159.
3. Gordon Allport, "The Productive Paradoxes of William James," *Psychological Review* 50 (1943):96.
4. *TC* 2:338.
5. Ibid., p. 583.
6. *SPP* pp. vii-viii.
7. *TC*, 2:96.
8. *PU*, pp. 250-51 (emphasis added).
9. *TC*, 2:53.
10. *Journal of Speculative Philosophy* 12 (1878):1-18, reprinted in *CER*.
11. *CER*, pp. 46, 52-53.
12. See for example in "The Sentiment of Rationality," *WB*, p. 92, "Pretend what we may, the *whole man* within us is at work when we form our philosophical opinions. Intellect, will, taste and passion cooperate just as they do in practical affairs."
13. *PP*, 1:1.

Chapter 2

1. *Psychology* was an abridgement of the former. James wrote of the shorter work that "about two-fifths of that volume is either new or rewritten, the rest is 'scissors and paste,' " and that it was written for purely commercial reasons. *TC*, 2:125.
2. *LWJ*, 1:294.
3. *PP*, 1:1.
4. Ibid., p. 5.
5. Ibid., p. 8 (emphasis added).
6. Cf. below.
7. *PP*, 1:185.
8. Ibid., p. 190.
9. Ibid., p. 193.
10. "The Mind and the Brain," *Nation* 24 (1877):356.
11. "Ladd's *Physiological Psychology*," *Nation* 44 (1887):473.
12. *TC*, 2:28.
13. Ibid., p. 96.
14. Cf. *Lectures on Immortality* (1898), in *WB*, pp. 1-31. Bruce Wilshire, *William James and Phenomenology* (Bloomington: Indiana University Press, (1968), especially pp. 30-67, argues that James never succeeds in explaining the causal connection between thought and the brain since he does not first specify (in terms of objects *known* in the world) what he means by thought.
15. *TC*, 2:53.
16. Ibid., p. 75 (emphasis added).
17. *PP*, 1:129.
18. James, "Are We Automata?" *Mind* 4 (1879):1.
19. Ibid., p. 3.
20. Ibid., p. 6.
21. *PP*, 1:141; and "Are We Automata?" pp. 6-7: "The words Use, Advantage, Interest, Good find no application in a

world in which no consciousness exists. Things are neither good or bad, they simply are or are not. Ideal truth to exist at all requires that a mind also exist which shall deal with it as a judge deals with the law, really creating what it professes only to declare."

22. *PP*, 1:144.
23. Ibid., p. 142.
24. Ibid., p. 144 and "Are We Automata?" p. 22. "Until then, I hold that we are incurring the slighter error by still regarding our conscious selves as actively combating each for his interests in the arena and not as impotently paralytic spectators of the game."
25. *TC*, 2:75.
26. *PP*, 1:224.
27. Cf. *TC*, 2:77. Note James' second claim does not rule out the ego because it is not empirically given but because it is pragmatically no different from "passing thought."
28. James, "Some Omissions in Introspective Psychology," *Mind* 9 (1884):10.
29. *PP*, 1:226.
30. Ibid., p. 291.
31. Ibid., p. 296.
32. Ibid., 2:298.
33. Ibid., p. 301.
34. Ibid., 1:305.
35. Ibid., pp. 319, 321.
36. *PSY*, p. 192.
37. Ibid., p. 200.
38. *PP*, 1:330.
39. *PSY*, p. 203.
40. *PP*, 1:339-40.
41. A. F. Bentley, "Truth, Reality and Behavioral Fact," *Journal of Philosophy* 40 (1943):169-87; idem, "The Jamesian Datum," *Journal of Psychology* 16 (1943):35-79.

42. John Dewey, "The Vanishing Self in the Psychology of William James," *Journal of Philosophy* 37 (1940):589-98.
43. Ibid., p. 597.
44. William James, *Journal of Philosophy, Psychology and Scientific Methods* 1 (1904):477-91, reprinted in *ERE*.
45. *PP*, 1:230.
46. Ibid., p. 234.
47. Ibid., p. 240.
48. James, "Some Omissions," p. 19.
49. *PP*, 1:221.
50. Ibid., p. 275.
51. Ibid., p. 139.
52. James, "Are We Automata?" p. 9.
53. *PP*, 2:2.
54. Besides the epistemological problem, recall James' physiological objection to identical, atomic sensations: this implies an unmodified brain state but our brain is constantly being modified by experience.
55. *PP*, 1:403.
56. Ibid., p. 444.
57. Ibid., 2:78.
58. Ibid., p. 78.
59. Ibid., p. 179.
60. Cf. *PP*, 2:82, 86; and William James, "Brute and Human Intelligence," *Journal of Speculative Philosophy* 12 (1878): 251, 256-57. The Gestalt strain in James' psychology is evident when he explains that we perceive the definite and probable thing since "all brain processes are such as give rise to *figured consciousness*," (*PP*, 2:82). The question of Jamesian vis à vis Gestalt Psychology is lengthy and complex; we will summarize only three points: James' anticipation of Gestalt psychology; Gestalt and Jamesian opposition to behaviorism; and differences between the two psychologies.

We have examined James' analysis of the perception of

undivided, articulated wholes and their subsequent discrimination of parts—a clear anticipation of the central Gestalt doctrine of perceptual configuration and their animus against atomistic psychology. James emphasized that the perceptual whole is not the summation of parts for the same sensation elements may yield different wholes, depending on the context or the feeling of the individual.

Although the Gestaltist and James understood the validity of conceiving the organism in the total situation of adjusting to environment, both nevertheless stress the importance of the *configurating individual*. In James' view, the efficacity of consciousness in interested selection is not the same as nor reducible to, sophisticated stimulus/response determinism.

The Gestaltists, wary of a timeless intellectual ego, neglected the integrating consciousness; James developed a theory of self in which passing thought, in space and time, is the conscious integrating self. Whereas Gestalt psychology is basically a psychology of perception, learning, and judgment, James emphasizes the emotional and volitional aspects of man. And finally, the Gestaltists stress the importance of perception of articulated *wholes*, while James is content with the *perceptual connectedness* gained through the substantive and transitive (especially the feelings of relation) states of consciousness.

61. *PP*, 2:103.
62. This chapter of *PP* was originally published as "The Psychology of Belief" *Mind*, 14 (1889):321-52.
63. Ibid., p. 297.
64. Ibid., p. 311.
65. Ibid., p. 317.
66. Ibid., 2:680.
67. Cf. *PP*, 2:348 ff. and James, "Brute and Human Intelligence," p. 238-43.
68. *PP*, 2:333.

69. Ibid., p. 333.
70. Ibid., p. 334 (emphasis added).
71. Ibid., p. 360.
72. Ibid., 1:482.
73. *PP*, 2:317.
74. Ibid., p. 334.
75. Ibid., p. 381.
76. This theory was advanced by James in an article "What Is an Emotion," *Mind* 9 (1884):188-205 (reprinted in *CER*), and almost simultaneously and independently by the Danish physiologist Carl Lange, hence it is usually called the James-Lange theory of emotions. For a discussion of James' originality in this regard see E. B. Tichner, "A Historical Note on the James-Lange Theory of Emotions," *American Journal of Psychology* 25 (1914):427-77.
77. *PP*, 2:450.
78. Ibid., p. 449.
79. Ibid., p. 467.
80. Ibid., p. 470.
81. Ibid., p. 383.
82. Ibid., p. 390.
83. Ibid., p. 393.
84. Ibid., p. 395.
85. In this connection see James' educational psychology: "The first thing, then, for the teacher to understand is the native reactive tendencies,—the impulses and instincts of childhood—so as to be able to substitute one for another, and turn them to artificial objects." *Talks to Teachers* (New York: W. W. Norton and Co., 1958), p. 22. For a survey of the native human instincts and their modification by society and education, cf. Ibid., pp. 20-32; *PP* 2:403-41; and *PSY*, pp. 406-14.
86. *PP*, 2:488 (emphasis added).
87. Ibid., pp. 498, 499 (emphasis added).

88. James, "The Feeling of Effort," (1880) Reprinted in *CER*, p. 154.
89. *PP*, 2:524.
90. Ibid., pp. 551, 527.
91. Ibid., p. 560.
92. Ibid., p. 567-68.
93. Cf. "The Feeling of Effort," *CER*, pp. 201-2: "If unpleasant consequences are expected, that effective sustaining of the idea which results in bringing the motion about and which is equivalent to mental consent that those consequences become real, involves considerable effort of volition. . . . The effort which the willing requires is the purely mental transition from the mere *conception* of the feelings to their *expectation*, steadfastly maintaining itself before the mind, disagreeable though it may be. The motor idea, assuming at last this victorious *status*, not only not inhibited by remote associations, but inhibited no longer even by its own unpleasantness, discharges by the preappointed mechanism into the right muscles. Then the motor sensations accrue in all their expected severity, and the *muscular* effort as distinguished from the volitional effort has its birth."

Chapter 3

1. This was the original title of his essay "The Moral Philosopher and the Moral Life."
2. Both are found in *WB*, "The Dilemma . . . ," pp. 145-83 and "The Moral Philosopher . . . ," pp. 184-215.
3. *LWJ*, 1:147.
4. *PP*, 2:567.
5. Ibid., p. 576.
6. *WB*, p. 150.
7. Ibid.

8. James' 1909 volume, *A Pluralistic Universe* is, in the main, a development of this train of thought. This will be treated at length in the next chapter.
9. *WB*, p. 161.
10. Ibid., p. 163.
11. Ibid., p. 164.
12. Ibid., p. 175.
13. James is careless with his terminology here but the two alternates are clear: evolutionists (sometimes called "empiricists") and intuitionists (sometimes called "apriorists").
14. *WB*, pp. 188-89.
15. *PP*, 2:618.
16. Ibid., p. 655.
17. Ibid., p. 659.
18. Ibid., p. 627.
19. Ibid., p. 672.
20. Ibid.
21. Ibid., p. 673.
22. *WB*, p. 199.
23. Ibid., p. 201.
24. John Dewey, *Essays in Experimental Logic* (Chicago: University of Chicago Press, 1916), pp. 35-36.
25. *WB*, p. 203.
26. Ibid., p. 205.
27. John F. Kennedy, *Profiles in Courage* (New York: Harper, 1956).
28. *PP*, 2:672.
29. *WB*, p. 212.
30. *VRE*, p. 423.
31. Ibid., p. 375.
32. The first, second and fourth articles are printed in *WB*, and the third was originally in *Mind* 14 (1889):321-52 and later in *PP*, 2:283-324.
33. *WB*, p. 11.

34. Included in vol. 14 of James' unpublished papers, released with the kind permission of the Houghton Library of Harvard and Mr. Alexander R. James. The article referred to in the letter is: Dickingson Miller, " 'The Will to Believe' and The Duty of Doubt," *International Journal of Ethics* 9 (1898-99):169-95.
35. *PP*, 2:312.
36. "Sentiment of Rationality," *Mind* 4 (1879):317. One of James' preoccupations was with what he called "the motives of philosophizing." In this regard, three articles are most informative, "The Sentiment of Rationality," Ibid., and "Rationality, Activity and Faith," *Princeton Review* 2 (1882):58-86. Both the above articles were combined into a single article, published in *WB*, and given the title "The Sentiment of Rationality." For clarity's sake, the last (i.e., revised) article will be referred to as "The Sentiment of Rationality—II."
37. James, "Sentiment of Rationality," p. 325.
38. Ibid., p. 326.
39. James, "Sentiment of Rationality—II," p. 77.
40. Ibid., p. 102.
41. Ibid., p. 110.
42. *WB*, p. 115.
43. Ibid., p. 141.
44. Ibid., p. 11.
45. Ibid., p. 8.
46. Ibid., p. 19.
47. In an extended treatment of this problem in "Is Life Worth Living," *WB*, pp. 32-62, James suggests that skepticism and neutrality would be commendable if life did not have to be lived by concrete action. Also, see his letter to Horace Kallen in *TC*, 2:249, "The question whether we have the right to believe anything before verification concerns not the constitution of truth, but the policy of belief. It is

usually poor policy to believe what isn't verified; but sometimes belief produces verification—as when it produces activity creative of the fact believed; and again, it may without altering given facts, be a belief in an altered meaning or value for them."

48. *WB*, p. 29. In order that the religious option be *forced* (based on a complete logical disjunction) the content of religious belief must be exhausted by its practical consequences. Accordingly, James' will to believe doctrine rests on two principles: that our passional natures control our beliefs and that the intellectual content of our beliefs is its practical effects. The only treatments of "The Will to Believe" which consciously distinguish these two principles are W. J. Macleod, "James' 'Will to Believe': Revisited." *Personalist* 48 (1967):149-66, R. B. Perry, *In the Spirit of William James* (New Haven: Yale University Press, 1938), pp. 201-3 and H. S. Thayer, *Meaning and Action: A Critical History of Pragmatism* (New York: Bobbs-Merrill, 1968), pp. 140-59. However, Macleod, Perry and Thayer have discussed at length only the second principle. Our analysis has been an extended treatment of the first principle. Our contention is that unless the first principle is understood properly, the second principle cannot be placed in the proper focus.

49. *VRE*, p. 31.

50. Ibid., p. 18.

51. Ibid., p. 35.

52. Ibid., p. 37.

53. James comments that although native temperament is a chief determinant of whether an individual will be healthy-minded or sick-souled, the outlook of the converted sick soul is philosophically superior. If religious experiences were evaluated solely on the basis of their effects on the believer ("congruence with our passional

natures") both religious outlooks would be equally satisfactory. However, two additional criteria are operative in
an evaluation of an experience: "factual evidence" (e.g.,
evil facts are as equally genuine and real parts of nature as
good facts) and "consistency with other beliefs" (e.g.,
genuine realities—here, evil—ought to be given a real
significance). The converted sick soul does not ignore evil
or explain it away but he appreciates its reality and deals
with it as such, hence the religious outlook in the converted sick soul is superior to that of the healthy-minded
believer.
54. *VRE*, p. 187.
55. Ibid., pp. 187-89.
56. Ibid., p. 196.
57. Ibid., p. 209.
58. Ibid., p. 207.
59. Ibid., p. 230.
60. Ibid., p. 242.
61. Ibid., p. 237.
62. Ibid., p. 331 (emphasis added).
63. Ibid., p. 375.
64. Ibid., p. 377.
65. Ibid., p. 373.
66. Ibid., p. 380.
67. Recall James' example of a blind man knowing *about* color
theory without being *acquainted* with color.
68. *VRE*, p. 381.
69. Ibid., p. 423.
70. Ibid., p. 427.
71. Ibid., p. 431.
72. Ibid., p. 445.
73. Ibid., p. 485.
74. Ibid., p. 505.
75. Ibid., p. 508.

76. Ibid.
77. "The word 'true' is here taken to mean something additional to the bare value for life, although the natural propensity of man is to believe that whatever has great value for life is thereby certified as true" (*VRE*, p. 509).
78. Ibid., p. 512.
79. Ibid., p. 515.
80. Ibid., p. 516-17.
81. Ibid., pp. 498-99.

Chapter 4

1. "Philosophical conceptions . . .," reprinted in *CER*, p. 410-11.
2. Ibid.
3. Ibid., p. 412.
4. Ibid.
5. C. S. Peirce, "The Fixation of Belief," *The Popular Science Monthly*, 1877; idem "How to Make Our Ideas Clear," *The Popular Science Monthly*, 1878. Reprinted in *The Collected Papers of C. S. Peirce* (Harvard University Press, Cambridge, 1934), pp. 223-71.
6. "The Pragmatic Method," *Journal of Philosophy* 1 (1904): 673-87.
7. *Mind* 13 (1904):457-75, reprinted in *MT*, pp. 51-101.
8. See, for example, almost any issue of *Mind* or *Journal of Philosophy* from 1907-10.
9. William Marra, in "The Five-sided Pragmatism of William James," *Modern Schoolman* 41 (1963-64):45-61, argues that the following orthodox position is held in common by Peirce, James, and Dewey: as a *theory of meaning*—we can make our ideas clear by enumerating the concrete, observable consequences which will result from a concept; as a *theory of truth*—the truth of a belief or an hypothesis

consists in the concrete, particular events which verify it, thus making it true.

10. As the reader may have noted, "idea," "word," "concept," and occasionally "belief" and "proposition" have been used interchangeably. Since James' intention was to explicate a method for getting clear about the meaning of *any* cognitive deliverance, he himself uses the above mentioned variety of terms to refer to those deliverances.

11. *Prag.*, p. 42.

12. *MT*, p. 52.

13. *Prag.*, p. 45.

14. In our second chapter, James argued that the mind guides future actions through the instrumentality of ideas which summarize, select, and reorganize past experience with a view to the needs and interests of the knower. Prominent among these needs is survival and accordingly this need is met by the "ascertainment of outward fact." However the other interests of the knower also determine the mind's activity: "The ascertainment of outward fact constitutes only one species of mental activity. The genus contains in addition to purely cognitive judgments . . . an immense number of emotional judgments: judgments of the ideal, judgments that things *should* exist thus and not so. How much of our mental life is occupied with this matter of a better or a worse?" ("Spencer's Definition of Mind," *CER*, p. 45). Hence for James, discussion of man's aesthetic, ethical, and religious interests insures that the "future consequences" of an idea need not be restricted to exclusively practical, survival-orientated consequences. For James, the meaning of an idea consists in the concrete experiences it leads to. Since these ideas may lead to experiences which may either satisfy or frustrate the interests which initiated the mind's activity, it is a short step to James' pragmatic theory of truth: ideas which lead to

satisfactory experiences are true, those which lead to frustration are false. James summarizes both theories: "The *pragmatic method* asserts that what a concept *means* is its consequences. *Humanism* (the pragmatic theory of truth) says that when these are satisfactory, the concept is true" (*TC*, 2:444).

15. *Prag.*, p. 43.
16. *CER*, p. 417.
17. Ibid., p. 423.
18. *Prag.*, p. 141.
19. Ibid., p. 133.
20. Ibid., p. 134.
21. Ibid., p. 140.
22. Ibid., p. 49.
23. Ibid., p. 50.
24. Ibid., p. 52.
25. Ibid., p. 151.
26. *MT*, pp. 94-95.
27. *Prag.*, p. 142.
28. *MT*, p. 72.
29. Ibid., p. 53.
30. *CER*, pp. 450-51.
31. *Prag.*, p. 159.
32. Ibid., pp. 157-74.
33. Ibid., p. 161.
34. *PP*, 2:334 (emphasis added).
35. *MT*, p. 58.
36. *Prag.*, p. 162 (emphasis added).
37. *MT*, p. 214.
38. *Prag.*, p. 167.
39. *MT*, pp. 92, 124.
40. Ibid., p. xii.
41. Ibid.
42. Expressed in a series of articles published in *The Journal*

of Philosophy, 1904-7, published posthumously as *Essays in Radical Empiricism* (New York: Longmans, Green and Co., 1917); also in his Hibbert lectures, *A Pluralistic Universe* (New York: Longmans, Green and Co., 1909); and, in another volume published posthumously, *Some Problems in Philosophy* (New York: Longmans, Green and Co., 1911).

43. *ERE*, p. 160.
44. Ibid., p. 95.
45. *MT*, p. xiii.
46. James generally referred to a portion or segment of "pure experience" as a "bit." Although he wished to avoid a term which would emphasize the atomic character of experience, he also sought to avoid a term which too strongly connoted the context-dependence of a portion of experience. In lieu of a solution to the problem of the self-identity yet context-dependence of a portion of the stream of pure experience, James resorted to using the vague term "bit." His interest was chiefly in explaining how a "bit" of pure experience could function in two different contexts. He distinguishes the two contexts by using various correlative terms: "subject/object," "knower/known," and "consciousness/content." Since no hard and fast rules were observed for the use of one or another set of correlatives, we have generally employed "knower/known" unless another set was used in a text.
47. *ERE*, pp. 93-94.
48. Ibid., p. 27.
49. Ibid., p. 23.
50. Ibid., p. 146.
51. *MT*, pp. 48-49.
52. Ibid., p. 50.
53. Ibid., pp. 44-45.
54. *ERE*, p. 60.
55. *MT*, pp. 142, 140.

56. *ERE*, p. 61.
57. *MT*, p. xv.
58. *ERE*, p. 160.
59. Ibid., p. 37.
60. This ambiguity is all the more remarkable when we notice that James' interest in the soul and psychical research spanned from an early review of a book on spiritualistic phenomenon in 1869, "Sargent's *Planchette*," to one of his last articles in 1909, "Final Impressions of a 'Psychical Researcher.' " Almost contemporaneously with this interest in the soul, James' affirmation that consciousness was simply awareness of cephalic movements spanned from "On Some Omissions in Introspective Psychology," (1884) to "Does 'Consciousness' Exist?", (1904).
61. *PU*, p. 289.
62. Ibid., p. 344, note no. 8.
63. Ibid., p. 288.
64. *CER*, p. 204.
65. *MT*, p. xiii.
66. This positive account of the structure of a pluralistic universe is contained in all his later works: *Prag.*, *MT*, *SPP*, and *ERE*.
67. *ERE*, p. 166.
68. *SPP*, p. 218.
69. *ERE*, p. 181.
70. Ibid., pp. 183-85.
71. Here "more rational" is understood in the full, concrete sense of rationality, explicated in "The Sentiment of Rationality."
72. *ERE*, p. 279.
73. *PU*, p. 13.
74. *SPP*, p. 141.
75. Ibid., p. 143.
76. Ibid.

77. *PU*, pp. 112, 113.
78. Ibid., p. 126.
79. Ibid., p. 73.
80. Ibid., p. 81.
81. Ibid., p. 351.
82. Ibid., p. 350.
83. The term "salvation" is never defined. James says of it only: "you may interpret the word 'salvation' any way you like, and make it as diffuse and distributive, or as climacteric and integral a phenomenon as you please" (*Prag.*, p. 185).
84. Ibid., p. 186.
85. Ibid., p. 187.
86. Ibid.
87. Ibid., p. 189.
88. Ibid., p. 192.
89. Ibid., p. 187.
90. See James' appendix to *SPP*, "Faith and the Right to Believe," pp. 223-24: "It may be true that work is still doing in the world process, and in that work we are called to bear our share. The character of the world's result may, in part, depend on our acts. Our acts may depend on our religion,— and on our not resisting our faith-tendencies, or on our sustaining them in spite of 'evidence' being incomplete. These faith-tendencies, in turn, are but expressions of our good-will toward certain forms of result."
91. *PU*, p. 311.
92. Ibid., p. 318.
93. Ibid., p. 124.
94. *VRE*, p. 517.

Chapter 5

1. *PP*, 1:8.
2. In addition, the other empirically given characteristics of

consciousness are that it is continuous, changing, and that it deals with things independent of itself.

3. *PP*, 2:551.

4. James observes that conscious states cause either inward bodily commotion (emotional reactions consequent upon sensation and perception) or outward bodily reaction (reflex and voluntary actions).

5. *PP*, 2:567-68.

6. *VRE*, p. 427.

7. "Without reservation" is not meant to imply that James fully resolved all the problems involved in his interactionist view of man. In our introduction, we pointed out that although he began his psychology by tentatively accepting an interactionist view of man, he only defined that view of man in reference to the conscious automaton theory. We noted that he had not then determined what "things" interact nor how they interact. In the development of his theory of man, he concluded that consciousness is efficacious (i.e., interacts), not by initiation (his phrase is "inwardly creating") but by selection. Further, he argues that a full, "spiritual" self, as the agent of selection is experienced in the exercise of our free will. Even though he did not establish a firm position on the specific nature of consciousness, he felt that the empirically given selectivity of consciousness and our experience of the full self warranted his acceptance of an interactionist view of man. His ambiguity on the precise nature of consciousness remains part of his legacy to American philosophy.

8. *Prag.*, p. 159.

9. *PP*, 2:334.

10. *Prag.*, p. 166.

11. *MT*, p. 214.

12. *SPP*, p. 214-15.

13. *PU*, p. 20.

14. *MT*, pp. 92, 124.
15. *Prag.*, p. 167.
16. *PU*, pp. 35-36.
17. Ibid., pp. 317-18.
18. *Prag.*, pp. 166-67.
19. *MT*, pp. 185-86 (emphasis added).
20. See *Prag.*, p. 147. "In the realm of truth—processes, facts come independently and determine our beliefs provisionally. But these beliefs make us act, and as fast as they do so, they bring into sight or into existence new facts which redetermine the beliefs accordingly. So the whole coil and ball of truth, as it rolls up, is the product of a double influence. Truths emerge from facts; but they dip forward into new facts again and add to them; these facts again create or reveal new truth and so on indefinitely."
21. "Humanism and Truth Once More," *Mind* 14 (1905): 192-93.
22. As defined, for example, by Wilson Coates, Hayden White and A. Salwin Schapiro in *The Emergence of Liberal Humanism* (New York: McGraw-Hill, 1966), p. 5: "[Humanism generally means] an attitude of mind which takes man as the effective qualitative center of the universe and as sole responsible agent for the creation of order in human affairs. . . . For a true humanism, such subjects as science, theology, and philosophy are far less important for what they tell us about their specifically designated objects of study than for what they tell us about man and his creative capabilities."

    James' philosophy is a humanism in the general sense of putting man in the central place of the whole of things. Also, James specifically refers to both the above positions. For example, on the former, see *SPP*, p. 214: "Human causal activity is the only known unconditional antecedent of the works of civilization." And in reference to the latter, recall his position in *VRE* that he is more interested in what religious experiences tell us about man than for what they tell us about God.

23. Quoted by Giuseppi Toffanin in *History of Humanism*, trans. Elio Gianturco (New York: Las Americas Publishing Co., 1954), p. 198. Although most scholars of humanism [for example, Ernst Cassirer, Paul Kristeller, and John Randall in *The Renaissance Philosophy of Man* (Chicago: University of Chicago Press, 1948), pp. 1-20, Frederick Artz in *Renaissance Humanism* (Oberlin, Ohio: Kent State University Press, 1966), pp. 87-93, and A. Robert Caponigri, *A History of Western Philosophy*, vol. 3 (Chicago: Henry Regnery, 1963): pp. 21-55] mention Marsilio Ficino and Giovanni Pico Della Mirandola as the classical loci for orations on the dignity of man, we have found Manetti more in accord with James' position. James and Manetti are concerned with the importance of human activity, thereby giving man his central place; whereas Ficino and Pico argue that man is the center of all things because man is a microcosm which shares in all things.

24. *Prag.*, p. 167.

Bibliography

SOURCES (THE WORKS OF WILLIAM JAMES IN SEQUENCE OF ORIGINAL PUBLICATION)

"Introduction" to *The Literary Remains of the Late Henry James*. 1884. 2d ed. Edited by William James. Boston: Houghton Mifflin Co., 1885.

The Principles of Psychology. 1890. Reprint 2 vols. New York: Dover Publications, 1950.

Psychology, the Briefer Course. 1892. 2d ed. New York: Henry Holt and Co., 1895.

The Will to Believe and Other Essays on Popular Philosophy and Human Immortality. 1897 and 1898. Reprint. New York: Dover Publications, 1956.

Talks to Teachers on Psychology: and to Students on Some of Life's Ideals. 1899. Reprint. New York: W. W. Norton and Co., 1958.

The Varieties of Religious Experience. 1902. Reprint. New York: Mentor Books, 1961.

Pragmatism and Four Essays from The Meaning of Truth. 1907 and 1909. Reprint. Cleveland: Meridian Books, 1963.

The Meaning of Truth, A Sequel to "Pragmatism." 1909. Reprint. New York: Longmans, Green and Co., 1928.

A Pluralistic Universe: Hibbert Lectures on the Present Situation in Philosophy. 1909. Reprint. New York: Longmans, Green and Co., 1932.

Some Problems of Philosophy. 1911. Reprint. New York: Longmans, Green and Co., 1931.

Memories and Studies. 1911. Reprint. New York: Longmans, Green and Co., 1928.

Essays in Radical Empiricism. New York: Longmans, Green and Co., 1920.

Collected Essays and Reviews. New York: Longmans, Green and Co., 1920.

The Letters of William James. Edited by his son Henry James. 2 vols. Boston: The Atlantic Monthly Press, 1920.

A bibliography of William James' uncollected essays and reviews can be found in Ralph Barton Perry's *Annotated Bibliography of the Writings of William James* (New York: Longmans, Green and Co., 1920).

STUDIES

Books

Abel, Ruben. *Humanistic Pragmatism: The Philosophy of F. C. S. Schiller.* New York: Free Press, 1966.

————. *The Pragmatic Humanism of F. C. S. Schiller.* Columbia University: King's Crown Press, 1955.

Allen, Gay Wilson. *William James: A Biography.* New York: Viking Press, 1967.

Artz, Frederick. *Renaissance Humanism, 1300-1550.* Oberlin: Kent State University Press, 1966.

Ayer, A. J. *The Origins of Pragmatism.* San Francisco: Freeman, Cooper and Co., 1968.

Bixler, Julius Seelye. *Religion in the Philosophy of William James.* Boston: Marshall Jones Co., 1926.

Blanshard, B., and H. Schneider, eds. *In Commemoration of William James, 1842-1942.* New York: Columbia University Press, 1942.

Boring, Edwin G. *A History of Experimental Psychology.* 2d ed. New York: Appleton-Century-Crofts, 1950.

Bradley, F. H. *Appearance and Reality.* Oxford: Clarendon Press, 1893.

_____. *Essays on Truth and Reality.* Oxford: Clarendon Press, 1914.

Brennan, Bernard P. *The Ethics of William James.* New York: Bookman Associates, 1961.

_____. *William James.* New York: Twayne Publishers, 1968.

Caponigri, A. Robert. *A History of Western Philosophy,* vol. 3. Chicago: Henry Regnery, 1963.

Cassirer, Ernst, Paul Kristeller and John Randall. *The Renaissance Philosophy of Man.* Chicago: University of Chicago Press, 1948.

Coates, Wilson; White, Hayden; and Schapiro, J. Salwin. *The Emergence of Liberal Humanism.* New York: McGraw-Hill, 1966.

Collins, James. *God in Modern Philosophy.* Chicago: Henry Regnery, 1959.

_____. *Three Paths in Philosophy.* Chicago: Henry Regnery, 1962.

Dewey, John. *Characters and Events.* 2 vols. New York: The Ad Press, Ltd., 1954.

_____. *Essays in Experimental Logic.* Chicago: University of Chicago Press, 1916.

_____. *On Experience, Nature, and Freedom.* Edited by Richard J. Bernstein. New York: Library of Liberal Arts, 1960.

_____. *The Influence of Darwin on Philosophy, and Other Essays in Contemporary Thought.* New York: Peter Smith, 1951.

_____.*Philosophy, Psychology, and Social Practice*. Edited by Joseph Ratner. New York: G. P. Putnam's Sons, 1963.

Ducasse, C. J. *A Philosophical Scrutiny of Religion*. New York: Ronald Press Co., 1953.

Fleigel, John. *A Hundred Years of Psychology*. New York: Basic Books, 1964.

Flournoy, Theodore. *The Philosophy of William James*. Translated by E. B. Holt and William James, Jr. New York: Henry Holt and Co., 1917.

Grattan, Clinton H. *The Three Jameses. A Family of Minds. Henry James, Sr., William James, and Henry James*. New York: New York University Press, 1962.

Hardwick, Elizabeth (ed.). *The Selected Letters of William James*. New York: Farrar, Straus and Cudahy, 1961.

Heidbreder, Edna. *Seven Psychologies*. New York: Appleton-Century-Crofts, 1961.

Hume, David. *A Treatise on Human Nature*. 2 vols. London: Longmans, Green and Co., 1909.

James, Henry. *The Letters of Henry James*. Edited by Percy Lubbock. 2 vols. New York: Charles Scribner's Sons, 1920.

_____.*Notes of a Son and Brother*. New York: Charles Scribner's Sons, 1914.

_____.*A Small Boy and Others*. New York: Charles Scribner's Sons, 1913.

Kallen, Horace M. *William James and Henry Bergson*. Chicago: University of Chicago Press, 1914.

Knox, Howard V. *The Philosophy of William James*. London: Constable and Co., 1914.

Konvitz, Milton R., and Kennedy, Gail, eds. *The American Pragmatists*. New York: Meridian Books, Inc., 1960.

Kristeller, Paul. *Eight Philosophers of the Italian Renaissance*. Stanford University Press, 1964.

Lapan, Arthur. *The Significance of James' Essay, "Does Consciousness Exist?"* New York: Law Printing Co., 1936.

LeClair, Robert, ed. *The Letters of William James and Theodore*

Flournoy. Madison: University of Wisconsin Press, 1966.

Linschoten, Hans. *On the Way Toward a Phenomenological Psychology: The Psychology of William James*. Translated by Amadeo Giorgi. Pittsburgh: Duquesne University Press, 1968.

Locke, John. *An Essay Concerning Human Understanding*. London: Clarendon, 1928.

Lovejoy, Arthur. *The Thirteen Pragmatisms and Other Essays*. Baltimore: Johns Hopkins Press, 1963.

Martland, T. R. *The Metaphysics of William James and John Dewey*. New York: The Philosophical Library, 1963.

Marx, Melvin, and Hillix, William. *Systems and Theories in Psychology*. New York: McGraw-Hill, 1963.

Matthiessen, F. O. *The James Family*. New York: Alfred Knopf, 1947.

Misiak, Henry, and Sexton, Virginia. *History of Psychology*. New York: Grune and Stratton, 1966.

Moore, Edward C. *American Pragmatism: Peirce, James, Dewey*. New York: Columbia University Press, 1961.

_____. *William James*. New York: Washington Square Press, Inc., 1965.

Morris, Lloyd R. *William James: The Message of a Modern Mind*. New York: Charles Scribner's Sons, 1950.

Muelder, W. G.; Sears, L.; and Schlabach, A., eds. *The Development of American Philosophy*. 2d ed. Boston: Houghton Mifflin Co., 1960.

Murphy, Gardner. *An Historical Introduction to Modern Psychology*. Rev. ed. New York: Harcourt, Brace, and Co., 1949.

_____, and Ballou, R. O., eds. *William James on Psychical Research*. New York: Viking Press, 1960.

Novak, Michael. *American Philosophy and the Future*. New York: Charles Scribner's Sons, 1968.

Peirce, Charles S. *Collected Papers of Charles Sanders Peirce*. Edited by C. Hartshorne, P. Weiss, and A. Burks. 8 vols. Cambridge: Harvard University Press, 1931-58.

_____. *Values in a Universe of Chance: Selected Writings of Charles S. Peirce.* Edited by Philip P. Wiener. Stanford: Stanford University Press, 1958.

Perry, Ralph Barton. *Annotated Bibliography of the Writings of William James.* New York: Longmans, Green and Co., 1920.

_____, ed. *Essays on Faith and Morals.* Cleveland: Meridian Books, 1962.

_____. *Philosophy of the Recent Past.* New York: Charles Scribner's Sons, 1926.

_____. *Present Philosophical Tendencies: A Critical Survey of Naturalism, Idealism, Pragmatism, and Realism with a Synopsis of the Philosophy of William James.* New York: Longmans, Green and Co., 1919.

_____. *In the Spirit of William James.* New Haven: Yale University Press, 1938.

_____. *The Thought and Character of William James.* 2 vols. Boston: Little, Brown and Co., 1935.

Ratner, Sidney and Jules Altman. *John Dewey and Arthur F. Bentley: A Philosophical Correspondence, 1932-1951.* New Brunswick: Rutgers University Press, 1964.

Renouvier, Charles. *Essais de Critique générale.* 5 vols. 2d ed., 1875-86. Reprint. Paris: Armand Colin, 1912. (Especially vols. iii-iv, *Traité de Psychologies rationelle.*)

Riley, Woodbridge. *American Thought from Puritanism to Pragmatism and Beyond.* 2d ed. New York: Peter Smith, 1941.

Roberts, James. *Faith and Reason: A Comparative Study of Pascal, Bergson and James.* Boston: The Christopher Publishing House, 1962.

Royce, Josiah. *William James and Other Essays on the Philosophy of Life.* New York: The Macmillan Co., 1911.

_____. *The World and the Individual.* 2 vols. New York: The Macmillan Co., 1900-1901.

Russell, Bertrand. *A History of Western Philosophy.* New York: Simon and Schuster, 1945.

Santayana, George. *Character and Opinion in the United States, with Reminiscences of William James and Josiah Royce.* New York: George Braziller, 1955.

Schiller, F. C. S. *Humanism: Philosophical Essays.* London: Macmillan, 1912.

_____. *Our Human Truths.* New York: Columbia University Press, 1939.

_____. *Studies in Humanism.* London: Macmillan, 1907.

Schneider, Herbert W. *A History of American Philosophy.* 2d ed. New York: Columbia University Press, 1963.

Smith, John E. *Religion and Empiricism.* Milwaukee: Marquette University Press, 1967.

_____. *The Spirit of American Philosophy.* New York: Oxford University Press, 1963.

Thayer, H. S. *Meaning and Action: A Critical History of Pragmatism.* New York: Bobbs-Merrill, 1968.

Toffanin, Giuseppe. *History of Humanism.* Translated by Elio Gianturco. New York: Las Americas Publishing Co., 1959.

Wild, John. *The Radical Empiricism of William James.* New York: Doubleday, 1969.

William James, the Man and the Thinker. Addresses Delivered at the University of Wisconsin in Celebration of the Centenary of His Birth. Madison: University of Wisconsin Press, 1942.

Wilshire, Bruce. *William James and Phenomenology: A Study of "The Principles of Psychology."* Bloomington: Indiana University Press, 1968.

Winetrout, Kenneth. *F. C. S. Schiller and the Dimensions of Pragmatism.* Ohio State University Press, 1967.

Articles

Allport, Gordon W. "The Productive Paradoxes of William James." *Psychological Review* 50 (1943):95-120.

Angier, Roswell. "Another Student's Impressions of James at the Turn of the Century." *Psychological Review* 50 (1943): 125-32.

Baum, Maurice. "The Attitude of William James Toward Science." *Monist* 42 (1932): 585-604.

———. "The Development of James' Pragmatism Prior to 1879." *Journal of Philosophy* 30 (1933):43-51.

Bentley, A. F. "The Jamesian Datum." *Journal of Philosophy* 16 (1943):35-79.

———. "Truth, Reality and Behavioral Fact." *Journal of Philosophy* 40 (1943):169-87.

Bixler, Julius S. "Mysticism and the Philosophy of William James." *International Journal of Ethics* 36 (1925):71-85.

Boring, Edward. "Human Nature vs Sensation: William James and the Psychology of the Present." *American Journal of Psychology* 55 (1942):310-27.

Bradley, F. H. "On the Ambiguity of Pragmatism." *Mind* 17 (1908):226-37.

Brotherston, B. W. "The Wider Setting of 'Felt Transitions'," *Journal of Philosophy* 39 (1942):97-104.

Bush, Wendell T. "William James and Panpsychism." In *Studies in the History of Ideas*. Vol. 2, pp. 313-26. New York: Columbia University Press, 1925.

Calkins, M. W. "Critical Comments on Gestalt." *Psychological Review* 33 (1926):135-38.

Cannon, W. B. "The James-Lange Theory of Emotions." *American Journal of Psychology* 39 (1927):106-24.

———. "James' Early Criticism of the Automaton Theory." *Journal of the History of Ideas* 15 (1954):260-79.

Capek, Milic. "The Doctrine of Necessity Re-examined." *The Review of Metaphysics* 5 (1951):11-54.

———. "The Reappearance of the Self in the Last Philosophy of William James." *Philosophical Review* 62 (1953):526-44.

Delabarre, Edmund. "A Student's Impressions of James in

the Late 90's." *Psychological Review* 50 (1943):134-36.

Dewey, John. "The Principles." *Psychological Review* 50 (1943): 121.

_____. "The Vanishing Subject in the Psychology of William James." *Journal of Philosophy* 37 (1940):589-99.

_____. "What Pragmatism Means by Practical." *Journal of Philosophy* 5 (1908):85-99.

Dooley, Patrick K. "The Nature of Belief: The Proper Context for James' 'The Will to Believe'." *Transactions of the C. S. Peirce Society* 8 (1972):141-51.

Fairbanks, Mathew. "Wittgenstein and James." *New Scholasticism* 40 (1966):331-40.

Fen, Sing-Nau. "Has James Answered Hume?" *Journal of Philosophy* 49 (1952):159-67.

Fisher, John. "Santayana and James: A Conflict of Views on Philosophy." *American Philosophical Quarterly* 2 (1965): 67-73.

Gurwitsch, Aron. "James' Theory of the 'Transitive Parts of the Stream of Consciousness'." *Philosophy and Phenomenological Research* 3 (1943):449-77.

Hare, Peter H., and Edward H. Madden. "William James, Dickinson Miller and C. J. Ducasse on the Ethics of Belief." *Transactions of the C. S. Peirce Society* 4 (1968):115-29.

Joseph, H. W. B. "Professor James on 'Humanism and Truth'." *Mind* 14 (1905):28-41.

Kallen, Horace M. "Remarks on Perry's Portrait of William James." *Philosophical Review* 46 (1937):71-78.

Kennedy, Gail. "Pragmatism, Pragmaticism, and the Will to Believe—A Reconsideration." *Journal of Philosophy* 55 (1958):578-88.

Kraushaar, O. F. "Lotze as a Factor in the Development of James' Radical Empiricism and Pluralism." *Philosophical Review* 48 (1939):455-71.

_____. "Lotze's Influence on the Pragmatism and Practical

Philosophy of William James." *Journal of the History of Ideas* 1 (1944):439-58.

———. "Lotze's Influence on the Psychology of William James." *Psychological Review* 43 (1936):235-57.

———. "What James' Philosophical Orientation Owed to Lotze." *Philosophical Review* 47 (1938):517-26.

Levinson, Ronald B. "A Note on One of James' Favorite Metaphors." *Journal of the History of Ideas* 8 (1947): 237-39.

———. "Sigwart's Logik and William James." *Journal of the History of Ideas* 8 (1947):475-83.

Lowe, V. "James and Whitehead's Doctrine of Prehensions." *Journal of Philosophy* 38 (1941):113-26.

Macleod, William J. "James' 'Will to Believe': Revisited." *Personalist* 48 (1967):149-66.

Madden, Edward. "Wright, James and Radical Empiricism." *Journal of Philosophy* 41 (1954):868-74.

Marra, William. "The Five-Sided Pragmatism of William James." *Modern Schoolman* 41 (1963-64):45-61.

Mavrodes, George I. "James and Clifford on 'The Will to Believe'." *Personalist* 44 (1963):191-98.

McCormick, John F. "The Pragmatism of William James." *The Modern Schoolman* 20 (1942-43):18-26.

McGeary, John K. "William James and the Modern Value Problems." *Personalist* 31 (1950):126-34.

McGilvary, E. G. "The Fringe in William James' Psychology: The Basis of Logic." *Philosophical Review* 20 (1911):144-56.

McTaggart, J. E. "Review of Pragmatism." *Mind* 17 (1908): 104-8.

Miller, D. S. "James' Doctrine of 'The Right to Believe'." *Philosophical Review* 51 (1942):541-58.

———. "James' Philosophical Development: Professor Perry's Biography." *Journal of Philosophy* 33 (1936):309-18.

———. "The Will to Believe and the Duty to Doubt." *International Journal of Ethics* 9 (1898-99):169-95.

_____,and Moore, J. S. "James' Doctrine of 'The Right to Believe'." *Philosophical Review* 52 (1943):69-70.

Nichols, Herbert. "The Cosmology of William James." *Journal of Philosophy* 19 (1922):673-83.

Otto, M. C. "On a Certain Blindness in William James." *Ethics* 52 (1942):184-91.

Perry, R. B. "James, the Psychologist as the Philosopher Sees Him." *Psychological Review* 50 (1943):122-24.

Pillsbury, W. B. "Tichner and James." *Psychological Review* 50 (1943):71-73.

Pratt, James B. "The Religious Philosophy of William James." *Hibbert Journal* 10 (1911):225-34.

Scheurtz, A. "The Concept of The Stream of Thought Phenomenologically Interpreted." *Philosophy and Phenomenological Research* 1 (1941):442-52.

Schiller, F. C. S. "Review of Pragmatism." *Mind* 16 (1907): 598-604.

Shouse, J. B. "David Hume and William James: A Comparison." *Journal of the History of Ideas* 13 (1952):514-27.

Sipfle, David A. "A Wager on Freedom." *International Philosophical Quarterly* 8 (1968):200-211.

Smith, John E. "Radical Empiricism." *Proceedings of the Aristotelian Society* 65 (1964-65):205-18.

Spoerl, Howard. "Abnormal and Social Psychology in the Life and Work of William James." *Journal of Abnormal and Social Psychology* 37 (1942):3-19.

Starbuck, Edwin. "A Student's Impressions of James in the Middle 90's." *Psychological Review* 50 (1943):132-34.

Thorndike, E. L. "James' Influence on the Psychology of Perception and Thought." *Psychological Review* 50 (1943):87-94.

Tichner, E. B. "A Historical Note on the James-Lange Theory of Emotion." *American Journal of Psychology* 25 (1914):427-47.

Weigand, Paul. "The Psychological Types of Frederich Schiller and William James." *Journal of the History of Ideas* 13 (1952): 376-83.

Wiggins, F. O. "William James and John Dewey." *Personalist* 23 (1942):182-98.

Wild, John. "James and Existential Authenticity." *Journal of Existentialism* 5 (1965):243-56.

Index

A

Adaptive behavior, 71-73
Agnosticism, 90-91
Aristotle, 118
Atheism, 90-91

B

Behaviorism, 35, 53-54
Belief, 47-49, 83-92
  common sense, 47-48
  guide to action, 91
  legitimacy of, 90-92, 109
  nature of, 84-89
  philosophies, 86-88
  religious, 88-92
  scientific theories, 85, 124-26
Bentley, A. F., 35

Berkeley, George, 118
Bradley, F. H., 95, 117
Bunyan, John, 96

C

Cause
  experienced as activity, 148, 155-56
  explanation of, 13, 17, 147-48, 184
Cephalic movements of adjustment; *see* Personal self
Clifford, W. K., 89-90
Conception, 49-52
Conscious automaton, 8-9, 26
Consciousness
  cognitive, 39-40
  constantly changing, 36-37

215

Consciousness (*continued*)
efficatious phenomenon, 20, 57-60
existence of, 143-144
impotent epiphenomenon, 20
selective; *see* Selectivity of consciousness
sensibly continuous, 37-38
stream of, 26-42
various descriptions of, 8-9
Conversion, 96-101
and the divided self, 99-101
gradual, 97-98
sudden, 98-99

D

Darwin, Charles, 51
De Dignitate Hominis, 178
Determinism
and freedom, 65-68
"hard and soft," 65
Dewey, John, 35, 75, 117
"The Dilemma of Determinism," 62, 64
"Does 'Consciousness' Exist" 35, 144

E

Emotion, 52-54
James-Lange theory of, 188

Essais de Critique Général, 55, 63
Essays in Radical Empiricism, 4, 55, 64, 82, 116, 132, 135, 144, 146, 160
Essential properties, non-existence of, 49-51
Ethics
casuistic question of, 74-79
James' theory of, 62-82
metaphysical question of, 63-74
psychological question of, 74-79
Evil, problem of, 149-52, 157-59; *see also* God as finite
"Evolutionists and Intuitionists," 69-74, 190
Experience
activity and novelty, 146-48
corrective of beliefs, 84-89, 91, 124-27, 131-32
"front and back door," 71-74, 166
"pure," 112-13, 135-40, 164, 197
reveals reality, 173-74

F

"The Feeling of Effort," 149
Freedom; *see* Novelty
"The Function of the Brain," 16

G

Genial and strenuous moods;
  see Philosophy and
  temperaments
Gestalt psychology, 186-87
God
  as finite, 157-59
  as an ideal moral companion,
    30-31
Goethe, Johann, 95

H

Hartmann, Nicolai, 86
Healthy-minded and sick-
  souled; *see* Philosophy
  and temperaments
Holt, Henry, 12
Human element, 1, 131, 154
Human Immortality, 4
Humanism, 1, 3, 107-13, 129-32
  classical meaning and James,
    175-79, 201-2
  and meliorism, 155-56
  philosophy of the human
    perspective, 174-75
  as a theory of truth, 172-73
"Humanism and Truth," 117
Hume, David, 26, 31, 38, 118

I

Illusion, 45-46
Instinct, 54-55

Interactionist view of man,
  7-9, 20-26, 36, 53, 93
Introspection, 15, 17

K

Kant, Immanuel, 26, 31, 38
Kennedy, John F., 77
Knowledge
  about, 39-40, 43, 136
  by acquaintance, 6, 39-40,
    43, 136, 139, 142
  perceptual and conceptual,
    140-43
  as a saltatory or ambulatory
    relation, 140-42, 160, 169

L

Leibnitz, Gottfried, 95
Locke, John, 118
Luther, Martin, 95

M

Manetti, Giannozzo, 178
Marcel, Gabriel, 137
The Meaning of Truth, 4, 113,
  122, 133
Meliorism, 68, 87-88, 126-27,
  154-58
  and human dignity, 175-79
Methodology of James, 3-7,
  93-94
  pragmatism as a, 116-21

Mind
    defined, 14, 19
    as a teleological instrument,
        50, 88-89, 118-20, 195-96
Monism, 149-53
Moore, G. E., 117
Moral experience and judg-
    ments of regret, 65-67
"The Moral Philosopher and
    the Moral Life," 62
Mysticism, 78-79, 104-6, 110-
    13, 168

N

Natural theology, 106-7, 110-
    13, 120
Nietzsche, Friedrich, 103
Novelty and freedom, 24, 61,
    63-68, 80, 146, 150-54,
    155
"Open" and "block uni-
    verse"; *see* Monism *and*
    Pluralism

P

Peirce, C. S., 83, 115-17, 119
Perception, 42-52
Personal self
    as cephalic movements, 29-
        30, 35-36, 144-45
    divided self, 99-101, 109-11
    as experienced, 143-46
    fluctuating boundaries,
        144-46

I, self as knower, 31-37
James' theory of, 27-36
me, self as known, 29-31
personal identity, 34
    as a structure of interests,
        30, 48, 51-52, 74, 146,
        167-69
    subconscious, 109-11, 164-70
    as substantial entity, 143-46,
        164-70
    as successive thoughts,
        33-34, 59
    various selves, 97-101
"Philosophical Conceptions
    and Practical Results," 116
Philosophy and temperaments
    genial and strenuous moods,
        77-79, 103-4, 157, 166-67
    healthy-minded and sick-
        souled, 94-96, 156, 192-93
    tough- and tender-minded,
        5, 119-20, 143-44, 171-72
Pluralism, 148-54
A Pluralistic Universe, 4, 25,
    36, 59, 64, 82, 113, 132,
    144, 146, 154, 160, 165, 170
Psychologist's fallacy, 15
Psychology
    a metaphysically neutral
        science of, 12, 16, 18-20,
        26, 36, 59, 164
    methods of, 14-20
    nature of, 16-20, 25
    scope of, 13-14

Psychology, 2, 4, 5, 11
"The Psychology of Belief," 83
Psychosomatic view of man;
   see Interactionist view of
   man
Practical
   actions, 90-91
   interests, 42, 46-47
Pragmatism, 2, 116-32
   as a humanism, 129-32
   orthodox, 117, 194
   and successfulness, 159
   as a theory of meaning, 117,
     118-21
   as a theory of truth, 117, 121
Pragmatism, 2, 4, 64, 113, 117,
   118, 122, 135, 140, 154, 179
"Pragmatism and Human-
   ism," 129
The Principles of Psychology,
   2, 4, 6, 11, 12, 13, 15, 16,
   17, 18, 62, 69, 74, 136
Profiles in Courage, 77

R

Radical empiricism, 115-16,
   133-61
   and solipsism, 142-43
Rationality
   the demands of, 86-88,
     151-55
   as a sentiment, 149

Reasoning, 49-52, 130
"Reflex Action and Theism,"
   83
Religious experiences, 63,
   94-113
   and ethics, 74-79, 102
   primal, 94-96
"Remarks on Spencer's
   Definition of Mind," 7
Renouvier, Charles, 55, 63
Rousseau, J. J., 95
Russell, Bertrand, 117

S

Saint Francis, 95
Sainthood, 78-79, 101-4, 168
Schiller, F. C. S., 4, 117, 129
Schopenhauer, Arthur, 66, 86
Scientific study of man, 12,
   16-19, 25-26, 28
Selectivity of consciousness,
   42-58
   and attention, 42, 44, 51
   and conception, 50
   and interests, 42, 44-46
Self, theory of; *see* Personal self
Sensation, 43-47
   and selection, 45-47, 130
"The Sentiment of Ration-
   ality," 83, 185
Some Problems of Philosophy,
   5, 149

Soul
  and knowing, 30-31
  and personal identity, 31-33
  as a substance, 59-60
Spencer, Herbert, 7, 14, 23
Spinoza, Baruch, 95
Stream of consciousness;
  see Consciousness

T

Talks to Teachers, 4
Theory of man, 6, 7
Tolstoi, Count Lev, 95, 96
Tough and tender minded;
  see Philosophy and
  temperaments

V

*The Varieties of Religious
  Experience*, 2, 4, 78, 82,
  92, 94, 103, 156, 157

Voluntary action, 55-59, 62,
  63; *see also* Novelty and
  freedom
  and experience of activity,
  147-48
  and psychic effort, 57-58,
  64, 189

W

Ward, James, 5, 17
Whole man, 7-9, 19, 24-26,
  59-60, 80, 92-93, 159, 161,
  169
  and the existence of the self,
  144-45
  as a guide to inquiry, 172
  and pluralism, 149-54
The Will to Believe, 2, 4, 82, 157
"The Will to Believe," James'
  doctrine of, 83-92